Gallbladder D[...]
Cookbook 2022

The Ultimate Gallbladder Guide with Proven, Delicious & Easy No Gallbladder Diet Recipes with Low Fat to Cleanse Your Body and Improve Your Health. 21 Day Action Plan Included.

Olivia Smith

Contents

Introduction

Step By Step Instructions For Dissolving Gallstones

Before we start looking at how to deal with gallstones, it's important to note that you should always defer to your doctor and follow their instructions over those that you read in a book. The information here is intended for general guidance, but does not take your personal medical situation into account, and therefore it should be treated as a secondary source, and not used to supersede the guidance of a medical practitioner.

A lot of experts currently agree that you do not need to treat gallstones unless they are causing you pain, but if you are finding that your gallstones are an issue, there are a few things you can try to combat them and help yourself live a pain-free life. Let's look at a few of the options that you have for dissolving gallstones without resorting to surgery.

Oral Dissolution Therapy

The first of these is oral dissolution therapy, which your doctor may prescribe to you. You will be given some pills that are made up of bile acid, and these can be used to successfully dissolve small stones in some cases.

It will rarely work on stones that are bigger than 1.5 cm in diameter, and it is most effective against those that contain a lot of cholesterol. This is not generally a very successful option, but it is an alternative to surgery and can be beneficial in some cases. If your doctor thinks that it may help you, they will suggest this course of treatment and prescribe the pills.

Take these according to your doctor's instructions, and your gallstones may be dissolved, either in full or in part. Note that it can take up to 2 years for these to have an effect, and they will not prevent new gallstones from forming. They are rarely prescribed for these reasons, but if they could help you, your doctor may suggest them.

Lose Weight

As with many other health issues, being overweight increases your risk of gallstones and obesity is a major risk factor for gallstone disease. Losing some weight and improving your diet is a good way to reduce your risk of developing gallstones, or at least of developing more. However, it is crucial to approach this sensibly.

It was originally thought that losing a lot of weight quickly could help with gallstones, but recent studies have shown that excessively fast weight loss can actually increase your risk instead. If you adopt a strict diet and shed a lot of weight at once, you might find yourself in greater danger of gallstones than if you remain overweight.

It is therefore critical that you follow a sensible plan for sustained and managed weight loss that will take place over a longer period. You should discuss your goals with your doctor to ensure that they are realistic, and make a plan for both your exercise and diet regime that you can follow. Losing around 1 or 2 pounds a week is generally considered a healthy approach, so avoid fad diets that claim that they can help you to lose more.

Try A Gallbladder Cleanse

It should be noted that so far, there is only anecdotal evidence to suggest that such cleanses are of any value to dissolving gallstones, and you should approach them with caution, because no studies back up their findings. Indeed, it is thought that some cleanses can be harmful and may cause digestive discomfort in various forms.

However, many people claim to have found such cleanses helpful, so you may wish to try one. You should discuss this with your doctor before you start to find out if there are any health implications in your circumstances.

Gallbladder cleanses usually involve consuming some fruit juice, olive oil, and herbs within the space of a few hours. This is thought to help break up the gallstones and encourage the gallbladder to release them. In theory, they can then be passed out of the body in urine.

However, because the evidence is currently limited to anecdotes, and you might give yourself cramps by performing this kind of cleanse, you should approach this method with caution. It is unlikely to do any harm, as the ingredients you will be consuming are all food safe, but you should be aware that it could make you uncomfortable and there may be no benefits to it. Some people claim that the "stones" released using this method are actually just lumps of juice and oil that have got mixed together in the system and released with the urine.

Until there are further studies to support the efficacy of cleanses, it may be best to avoid them. If you are on any medication, it is particularly important to discuss the idea of a cleanse with your doctor.

Milk Thistle

Milk thistle has been used for centuries to support the liver and it is also thought to benefit the gallbladder's function. However, there is not yet any evidence that it can dissolve the stones once they have formed, so again, you should treat this method with caution.

There is unlikely to be any harm in trying this, but you may wish to consult your doctor before you do, especially if you are diabetic, allergic to ragweed, or have other health complications.

Overall, there are not many known ways to dissolve gallstones once they have formed. This is unfortunate and frustrating, and has led to people trying a wide variety of at-home cures, but unless the medication listed above is able to help, your best option is to work to avoid further stones forming. You can do this in a multitude of ways, and particularly by improving your diet and getting yourself to a healthy weight.

How To Improve Your Gallbladder Function So Your Digestive System Functions Properly

There are numerous things that you can do to support your gallbladder and improve your digestive function, and this can take pressure off the organ and make you more comfortable if you are suffering from issues. Indeed, some of these are things that anyone will benefit from doing, and they will lower your risk of getting gallstones, or getting more gallstones.

Eat More Vegetables For Fibre And Protein

Fibre is one of the keys to keeping your digestive system healthy because it ensures that food moves through your guts swiftly and effectively. You can get fibre from wholegrain foods, such as wholemeal pasta, brown rice, brown bread, etc. Other forms of food that have fibre in them are fruits and vegetables, so the more of these you eat, the better your digestive system should function.

You should make an active effort to include more fibre in your diet by meal planning and consciously noticing which meals do not contain much. Make efforts to swap to the wholemeal versions of your favourite foods at least some of the time, and avoid white bread, white pasta, etc.

Plant-based foods tend to be high in fibre, and it is thought that they offer the best chance of creating a diet that will boost your gallbladder function and minimise your risk of disease. A study done in 2016 found a link between the increased intake of vegetable protein and the decreased risk of gallbladder disease.

Eat Regularly

Regular meals will also be helpful to your guts, and should keep everything moving nicely, putting less pressure on the gallbladder. You are more likely to eat moderate, manageable amounts if you eat frequently. Fasting is growing in popularity, but it is something that you should discuss with your doctor before undertaking if you are concerned about your gallbladder.

Most experts recommend regular, small meals or light, healthy snacks throughout the day to keep your digestive system operating and ensure that your gallbladder is releasing bile to help with digestion on a regular basis.

Opt For Healthy Fats

Experts no longer recommend cutting all the fat out of your diet; instead, they suggest choosing healthy fats that will encourage your gallbladder to contract and release the bile it is holding frequently. Remember that your gallbladder holds onto bile while you are not eating, and releases it when you consume something fatty to help break down the fats and make them easier to digest.

By choosing healthy oils such as fish oil and olive oil, you will ensure that the gallbladder is regularly contracting, releasing bile, and emptying itself. This decreases your risk of gallstones and should improve your digestion.

Avoid Sugary And Fatty Foods

Apart from the inclusion of healthy fats, you should try to cut back on how much fat you eat, because this will help you to get in control of your weight and become healthier. Reducing the amount of sugar in your diet will also make it easier to lose weight, lowering your risk of gallstones.

This means removing many things like pastries, sugary desserts, sweet cakes, chocolate, and fried food from your diet, or at least cutting back on them. Refined carbohydrates, sugar, and unhealthy fats should be avoided as far as possible so that your digestive system can function properly and your gallbladder is kept healthy.

Get To A Healthy Weight

As mentioned above, being at a healthy weight is a critical aspect of reducing your gallstone risk, and you need to do everything that you can to achieve and maintain a healthy body weight. You should discuss the realities of this with your medical practitioner to make sure that you choose a safe approach to weight loss, but cutting down on your weight is a critical part of improving your gallbladder function and can reduce your risk of gallstones.

Drink Coffee

There is some evidence that indicates coffee could improve the functionality of your gallbladder. It is thought to balance the chemicals and stimulate the activity of this organ, as well as the activity of the intestines. This could make your digestive system work better, and ensure that the gallbladder is doing its job effectively.

More research is needed for us to fully understand how the gallbladder's functioning can be improved through these methods, but the above tips should help you get started, and may make the whole digestive process more comfortable for you. Talk to your doctor about them before making a start so that any changes to your health can be monitored.

How To Manage Gallbladder Attacks

If you are suffering from a gallbladder attack, you will be in pain, and this is more likely to happen in the evening when you have eaten a large meal. The symptoms may not be serious, but you should be cautious about self-medicating to mask the pain, and instead seek medical advice. There are things you can do to reduce the discomfort, although it is best to discuss these with a doctor before employing them.

Unfortunately, gallbladder attacks can be unique to each individual, and what works for one person could make the symptoms worse for another. You may wish to try the below suggestions to see if any are effective for you.

Peppermint Tea

Often used to deal with stomach upsets, peppermint tea will help to soothe gallbladder attacks for some people. This is because of the menthol in it, which promotes pain relief and can naturally ease discomfort in your abdomen. It is also possible for it to improve your digestion overall, making you more comfortable.

Magnesium

Magnesium is thought to play a role in encouraging the gallbladder to empty properly, and being deficient in magnesium could play a role in the formation of gallstones. That means you may wish to start taking a supplement; this should be discussed with your doctor to ascertain what the appropriate dose may be. Alternatively, try to include plenty of magnesium-rich foods (such as nuts) in your diet.

Heat

You may find that applying heat to your abdomen eases the pain caused by a gallbladder attack. You can make a hot water bottle and wrap it in a towel, or apply a heating pad or a hot, wet towel. Hold it in place against the area that is painful for up to 15 minutes, being careful not to burn your skin in the process. This may help to ease the discomfort without you needing to take any medication.

Apple Cider Vinegar

Some individuals find that sipping diluted apple cider vinegar helps to reduce the discomfort of a gallbladder attack. To try this, dilute a couple of tablespoons of vinegar with some warm water, and sip it gradually. It has anti-inflammatory properties that may help to ease the pain. However, you should avoid drinking it neat; always dilute it, or you may damage your teeth and cause stomach pain.

There is no guarantee that you will find these methods effective against a gallbladder attack, so it's a good idea to determine what prompts the attacks and how you can avoid them, as well as having some remedies for them. If you find that eating a large meal before you go to bed is causing the problem, try reducing the portion size, cutting out some of the fat, or having a snack and a smaller meal over the course of the evening. This may help to lower the risk of the attack happening at all.

How To Save Your Gallbladder With Safe, Natural Remedies

You might be wondering whether you can turn to natural remedies to help treat your gallbladder problems and improve the health of this organ, but you should be careful if you plan to do so. While certain natural remedies may be able to help when you are suffering from a gallbladder attack, there is currently little scientific evidence to support the efficacy of these remedies. Always discuss natural treatments with your doctor before you start using them, to mitigate the risk of any issues occurring.

Some natural remedies that are suggested include the following:

Carrot Juice

Carrot juice is particularly high in vitamin C, and it is thought that vitamin C consumption can minimise the deposits of calcium. These deposits lead to stone formation, so taking carrot juice may reduce the risk of stones forming. The juice may also clean up your gastrointestinal system and could stimulate bile production, stopping bile from forming into stones.

Fennel

If you enjoy fennel, you might be pleased to learn that it could also contribute to the health of your gallbladder. It is thought to reduce inflammation, so try cooking with it, or try drinking fennel tea. Neither of these things is likely to have a massive impact on the health of your gallbladder, but they could be beneficial, and they are certainly worth trying if you are concerned.

Ginger

Ginger is a popular remedy for all kinds of complaints, and if you are suffering from health issues, you might want to start incorporating more ginger into your diet. You can do this in the form of tea, baking (although be wary of increasing your sugar intake), or crystallised ginger if you prefer.

Ginger helps because it converts cholesterol into bile acids, and this can again reduce the risk of stones forming. Try incorporating ginger in your meals on a regular basis for maximum effect.

Berries

Fruits that are high in vitamin C are a good alternative to carrot juice if you aren't fond of it (or if you want to supplement it). Taking plenty of vitamin C could reduce your overall risk of gallbladder disease, and being deficient in vitamin C might increase your cholesterol levels. Consequently, you should try eating strawberries, blackberries, and kiwis, or other fruits that are rich in vitamin C.

Avoid Heavy Dieting

As mentioned earlier, losing weight can be a good way to reduce your risk of gallbladder disease, but only if you do so in a controlled and gradual manner. That means you should avoid any crash diets or stringent diets that are focused on fast weight loss. Losing too much weight too fast will stop your gallbladder from emptying as it should, and this will increase the risk of gallstones forming.

If you are going to diet, make sure that you are doing so in a gradual, sustainable way, preferably approved by a doctor. This will reduce the stress on your organs and ensure that your body has time to adjust to the changes.

Alcohol

Although you should only ever drink alcohol in moderation and you absolutely should not binge on alcohol in an attempt to repair damage to your gallbladder, some studies indicate that including a small amount of alcohol in your diet can reduce your risk of gallbladder problems. It can raise the levels of HDL (good) cholesterol in the blood, which may have a positive effect on bile. However, alcohol can damage your gallbladder if it is drunk in large quantities, so limit yourself to 1 glass of alcohol per day (women) or 2 glasses (men). Avoid heavy spirits, and stick to wine or beer.

Nuts

Nuts are thought to be very good for your overall health because they contain healthy fats and lots of plant fibre. They can be an ideal food if you are concerned about the health of your gallbladder. It is thought that eating nuts can reduce your risk of absorbing cholesterol, and may significantly reduce the chances of you developing problems with your gallbladder.

Water

Staying hydrated is a key to managing your digestion well and keeping all the organs involved in digesting your food healthy. Water is thought to help the gallbladder empty its bile out, preventing a build-up and reducing the risk of stones forming. You should therefore make sure that you are staying hydrated throughout the day. Don't just drink with meals, or try to gulp down as much water as possible during the rare moments you think about it. Instead, sip water throughout the day to keep your body hydrated. You may find that it helps to buy a water bottle that measures your daily requirement, but be aware that this requirement does vary from person to person, and you don't need to force yourself to drink if you genuinely aren't thirsty.

With all of these remedies, bear in mind that more study is needed to confirm their efficacy, and you should always turn to your doctor for information before you try something. These are considered safe in most cases (unless you have allergies or other health conditions that prevent you from eating certain foods), and they should not harm you, but it's still wise to check in with your healthcare professional before you make major changes to your diet.

Everything You Need To Know About Gallbladder Surgery

If you are facing gallbladder surgery, you might be feeling nervous, but be aware that this is generally fairly minor and can be a good way to resolve any problems associated with your gallbladder.

Gallbladder surgery is often known as a cholecystectomy, and it can be undertaken in two different ways:

- You can have keyhole surgery, where you have several small cuts made in your stomach so that surgical instruments can enter and remove your gallbladder

- You can have an open cholecystectomy, which involves making one larger incision so that the gallbladder can be removed

Both of these methods will be undertaken under a general anaesthetic so you will be unaware of the operation, and you will not feel any pain. You may need someone to drive you home from the hospital afterwards. In general, keyhole surgery is favoured because it reduces the recovery time and results in less scarring, but either surgery can be performed, and both are safe and effective methods for treating gallbladder issues.

As with any kind of surgery, there are some risks, and these include:

- Blood clots

- Wound infections

- Bile leaking into the tummy

- Damage to one of the ducts that transport bile out of the liver

However, most of these are considered low risk and your doctor should discuss them with you – along with the benefits of gallbladder surgery – prior to booking anything.

If you have had keyhole surgery, you will usually have fully recovered enough from the surgery to leave either the same day or the following day, and you should then rest for a few days. You will probably be able to resume normal activity levels within a couple of weeks.

For open surgery, anticipate a longer period of recovery. It may be between 3 and 5 days before you can leave the hospital, and then it could be a month and a half or 2 months before you start to feel normal again. Follow your doctor's advice regarding what level of exercise and activity you should undertake at this time to ensure you do not set back your recovery.

How To Live A Healthy Life Without A Gallbladder

It is perfectly possible to live a healthy life without your gallbladder, and many people do. This organ is not crucial to your survival, and you will not need a medical aid to replace it. Bile production will continue in your liver; there just won't be anywhere to store it.

This means that the bile will drip into the digestive system, rather than being collected up and then released. Fortunately, this rarely causes any problems, and there is no need to prevent it from happening. You may have some issues with diarrhoea or bloating for a few weeks following the surgery, but this will usually balance out as your body adjusts.

You might be wondering whether you will need to follow a special diet after your gallbladder has been removed, and the answer is that most people do not need to. In general, you can return to your normal diet a few hours after the operation, starting with some small meals so that your system has time to adjust.

If you have been advised to follow a low fat diet prior to the surgery, there is no need to continue this afterwards. You should instead start incorporating some healthy fats back into your diet, making sure that you maintain a balance with other foods too. Keep your meals small and work on implementing as much balance as possible, so that you remain a healthy weight and your digestive system operates smoothly.

If you are encountering issues such as indigestion, diarrhoea, bloating, or other problems, you should try some of the following steps to mitigate the problem:

- Increase your fibre intake slowly so that you are eating more nuts, wholegrain breads, wholemeal pastas, and lots of fruits and vegetables. Do not add too many fibre-rich foods to your plate at once, as this can cause more problems, but work to gradually increase the amount of fibre you consume.

- Cut down on the number of caffeinated drinks that you consume, or drop them from your diet entirely.

- Go easy on spicy and fatty foods, as these may make the issues worse. You do not have to remove them from your diet altogether, but reduce your intake and be aware that they may cause more issues than they might have previously.

You should also exercise caution with any foods that you have noticed triggered problems in the past. If certain foods set off attacks or cause discomfort and bloating, avoid these or remove them from your diet. This should leave you feeling happier and healthier overall.

Note that if you have had other kinds of surgery and other organs removed, you may need to adapt your diet to fit your conditions, but with gallbladder surgery, most people can resume eating a normal, healthy diet after the surgery has been completed. If you are suffering from ongoing symptoms after several weeks have passed, consult your doctor for advice on how to further mitigate them, or for medication that can help

Breakfast Recipes

Fruity Chia Pudding

Servings|4   Time|10 minutes
Nutritional Content (per serving):
Cal| 158   Fat| 6.3g   Protein| 5.4g   Carbs| 25.9g   Fibre| 9.8g

Ingredients:

- 180 millilitres (¾ cup) unsweetened almond milk
- 5 large soft dates, pitted and chopped
- 150 grams (1 cup) frozen blueberries
- ½ of frozen banana, peeled and sliced
- 80 grams (½ cup) plus 10 grams (1 tablespoon) chia seeds

Directions:

1. Add all ingredients in a food processor except for chia seeds and pulse until smooth.
2. Transfer the mixture in a bowl.
3. Add chia seeds and stir to combine well.
4. Refrigerate for 30 minutes, stirring after every 5 minutes.

Overnight Oatmeal

Servings|2   Time|10 minutes
Nutritional Content (per serving):
Cal| 245   Fat| 4.3g   Protein| 7g   Carbs| 44.8g   Fibre| 6.7g

Ingredients:

- ❖ 100 grams (1 cup) gluten-free rolled oats
- ❖ 15 grams (2 teaspoons) honey
- ❖ 40 grams (¼ cup) fresh blueberries
- ❖ 2½ grams (½ teaspoon) ground cinnamon
- ❖ 240 millilitres (1 cup) unsweetened almond milk

Directions:

1. In a large bowl, add all ingredients except for blueberries and mix until well combined.
2. Cover the bowl and refrigerate overnight.
3. In the morning, top with blueberries and serve.

Yoghurt Oatmeal

Servings|2   Time|10 minutes
Nutritional Content (per serving):
Cal| 244   Fat| 3g   Protein| 12.2g   Carbs| 43.3g   Fibre| 6.2g

Ingredients:

- ❖ 480 millilitres (2 cups) water
- ❖ 200 grams (7 ounces) fat-free plain Greek yoghurt
- ❖ 40 grams (¼ cup) fresh blueberries
- ❖ 100 grams (1 cup) gluten-free old-fashioned oats
- ❖ 1¼ grams (¼ teaspoon) ground cinnamon

Directions:

1. In a saucepan, add the water over medium heat and bring to a boil.
2. Stir in the oats and cook for about 5 minutes, stirring occasionally.
3. Remove the pan of oats from the heat and stir in half of the yoghurt and cinnamon.
4. Divide the oatmeal into serving bowls evenly.
5. Top each bowl with the remaining yoghurt and blueberries and serve

Apple Porridge

Servings|4   Time|15 minutes
Nutritional Content (per serving):
Cal| 151   Fat| 7.3g   Protein| 3g   Carbs| 18.5g   Fibre| 4.1g

Ingredients:

- 480 millilitres (2 cups) unsweetened almond milk
- 2 large apples, peeled, cored and grated
- Pinch of ground cinnamon
- 20 grams (3 tablespoons) unsalted walnuts, chopped
- 25 grams (3 tablespoons) unsalted sunflower seeds
- 2½ millilitres (½ teaspoon) organic vanilla extract

Directions:

1. In a large saucepan, mix together the milk, walnuts, sunflower seeds, grated apple, vanilla and cinnamon over medium-low heat and cook for about 3-5 minutes.
2. Remove from the heat and serve warm.

Buckwheat Porridge

Servings|4   Time|10 minutes
Nutritional Content (per serving):
Cal| 348   Fat| 4.1g   Protein| 11.4g   Carbs| 68.6g   Fibre| 11g

Ingredients:

- ❖ 340 grams (2 cups) buckwheat groats
- ❖ 20 grams (2 tablespoons) chia seeds
- ❖ 5 grams (1 teaspoon) ground cinnamon
- ❖ 360 millilitres (1½ cups) unsweetened almond milk
- ❖ 5 millilitres (1 teaspoon) organic vanilla extract
- ❖ Pinch of sea salt
- ❖ 75 grams (½ cup) fresh blueberries

Directions:

1. In a bowl of water, soak the buckwheat groats overnight.
2. Drain the buckwheat groats and rinse well.
3. Again, drain the buckwheat groats completely.
4. Place the buckwheat groats, almond milk, chia seeds and vanilla extract in a food processor and pulse until well combined.
5. Add the cinnamon and salt and pulse until smooth.
6. Serve immediately with the topping of blueberries.

Tomato & Egg Scramble

Servings|4   Time|16 minutes
Nutritional Content (per serving):
Cal| 187   Fat| 9.3g   Protein| 17g   Carbs| 2.9g   Fibre| 0.6g

Ingredients:

- 30 millilitres (2 tablespoons) olive oil
- 2 jalapeño peppers, finely chopped
- 85 grams (3 ounces) low-fat cheddar cheese, shredded
- Pinch of sea salt
- 1 tomato, finely chopped
- 1 green onion (scallion), finely chopped
- 12 egg whites, beaten
- Ground black pepper, as required

Directions:

1. In a large frying pan, heat olive oil over medium-high heat and cook the tomato, green onion (scallion), and jalapeños for about 3-4 minutes, stirring frequently.
2. Add the beaten egg whites and cook for about 2 minutes, stirring continuously.
3. Stir in the cheese, salt, and black pepper, and remove from the heat.
4. Serve hot.

Tomato Omelet

Servings|2 Time|16 minutes
Nutritional Content (per serving):
Cal| 146   Fat| 6.3g   Protein| 15.3g   Carbs| 3.7g   Fibre| 1g

Ingredients:

- 8 large egg whites
- Ground black pepper, as required
- ¾ gram (1/8 teaspoon) ground turmeric
- 2 green onions (scallions), finely chopped
- Pinch of sea salt
- 15 millilitres (1 tablespoon) olive oil
- 1¼ grams (¼ teaspoon) mustard seeds
- 45 grams (¼ cup) cherry tomatoes, chopped

Directions:

1. In a bowl, add egg whites, salt and black pepper and beat well. Set aside.
2. In a cast iron wok, heat oil over medium-high heat and sauté turmeric and mustard seeds for about 30 seconds.
3. Add scallion and sauté for about 30 seconds.
4. Add tomatoes and cook for about 1 minute.
5. Add the egg mixture in the wok evenly and cook for about 2 minutes.
6. Carefully tilt the pan and cook for about 2 minutes more.
7. Transfer the omelet into a plate and cut into 2 wedges.
8. Serve hot with the sprinkling of black pepper.

Spinach Omelet

Servings|2   Time|16½ minutes
Nutritional Content (per serving):
Cal| 131   Fat| 6.3g   Protein| 12.4g   Carbs| 2.9g   Fibre| 0.6g

Ingredients:

- 4 large egg whites
- 2 green onions (scallions), chopped
- 55 grams (½ cup) low-fat feta cheese, crumbled
- 10 millilitres (2 teaspoons) olive oil
- 10 grams (¼ cup) fresh spinach, finely chopped
- 5 grams (2 tablespoons) fresh parsley, chopped
- Ground black pepper, as required

Directions:

1. Preheat the broiler of oven. Arrange a rack about 10-centimetre (4-inch) from heating element.
2. In a mixing bowl, add all ingredients except for oil and stir to combine.
3. In an ovenproof wok, heat olive oil over medium heat.
4. Add egg mixture and tilt the wok to spread the mixture evenly.
5. Immediately, adjust the heat to medium-low and cook for about 3-4 minutes or until golden-brown.
6. Now, transfer the wok under broiler and broil for about 1½-2½ minutes.
7. Cut the omelet into desired size wedges and serve.

Tuna Omelet

Servings|2 Time|20 minutes
Nutritional Content (per serving):
Cal| 229   Fat| 7g   Protein| 33g   Carbs| 4.3g   Fibre| 0.8g

Ingredients:

- 8 egg whites
- 5 grams (1 tablespoon) green onion (scallion), chopped
- ½ of jalapeño pepper, minced
- Ground black pepper as required
- 15 millilitres (1 tablespoon) olive oil
- 30 grams (3 tablespoons) capsicum (bell pepper) seeded and chopped
- 60 millilitres (¼ cup) unsweetened almond milk
- 1 garlic clove, minced
- Pinch of sea salt
- 1 (140-gram) (5-ounce) can water-packed tuna drained and flaked
- 40 grams (3 tablespoons) tomato, chopped

Directions:

1. In a bowl, add the eggs, almond milk scallions, garlic, jalapeño pepper, salt, and black pepper, and beat well.
2. Add the tuna and stir to combine.
3. In a large-sized cast-iron frying pan, heat oil over medium heat.
4. Place the egg mixture in an even layer and cook for about 1–2 minutes, without stirring.
5. Carefully lift the edges to run the uncooked portion flow underneath.
6. Spread the veggies over the egg mixture and sprinkle with the cheese.
7. Cover the frying pan and cook for about 30-60 seconds.
8. Remove the lid and fold the omelet in half.
9. Remove from the heat and cut the omelet into 2 portions.
10. Serve immediately.

Banana Pancakes

Servings|6   Time|1 hour 4 minutes
Nutritional Content (per serving):
Cal| 169   Fat| 6g   Protein| 4.8g   Carbs| 25g   Fibre| 2.2g

Ingredients:

- 100 grams (1 cup) gluten-free rolled oats
- 75 grams (¼ cup) maple syrup
- 5 millilitres (1 teaspoon) organic vanilla extract
- 30 millilitres (2 tablespoons) water
- 4 egg whites
- 1 ripe banana, peeled
- 30 millilitres (2 tablespoons) olive oil
- 8 grams (2 teaspoons) baking powder

Directions:

1. In a high-power blender, add all the ingredients and pulse until smooth.
2. Transfer the oatmeal mixture into a bowl.
3. Heat a greased non-stick wok over medium heat.
4. Place desired amount of the mixture and with a spatula, spread in an even circle.
5. Cook for about 4-5 minutes.
6. Flip and cook for about 3-4 minutes.
7. Repeat with the remaining mixture.
8. Serve warm.

Chicken Pancakes

Servings|4   Time|47 minutes
Nutritional Content (per serving):
Cal| 74   Fat| 4.2g   Protein| 5.4g   Carbs| 4.9g   Fibre| 1.7g

Ingredients:

- ❖ 460 grams (4 cups) courgettes (zucchinis), shredded
- ❖ 25 grams (¼ cup) green onion (scallion), finely chopped
- ❖ Ground black pepper, as required
- ❖ 30 grams (¼ cup) cooked chicken, shredded
- ❖ 2 egg whites, beaten
- ❖ 25 grams (¼ cup) coconut flour
- ❖ 15 millilitres (1 tablespoon) olive oil

Directions:

1. In a colander, add zucchini and sprinkle with salt.
2. Set aside for about 8-10 minutes.
3. Squeeze the zucchinis well and transfer into a bowl.
4. In a bowl, add squeezed courgette (zucchini) and remaining ingredients and mix until well combined.
5. In a large non-stick wok, heat oil over medium heat.
6. Add desired amount of courgette (zucchini) mixture into the preheated wok and spread in an even layer.
7. Cook for about 3-4 minutes per side.
8. Repeat with the remaining mixture.
9. Serve warm.

Spinach Pancakes

Servings|8   Time|1 hour 1 minute
Nutritional Content (per serving):
Cal| 100   Fat| 6.3g   Protein| 3.2g   Carbs| 3.2g   Fibre| 1.5g

Ingredients:

- 4 egg whites
- 2 grams (½ teaspoon) baking powder
- 30 grams (1 cup) fresh spinach, chopped
- 1 garlic clove, chopped
- 1¼ grams (¼ teaspoon) ground nutmeg
- Pinch of sea salt
- 100 grams (1 cup) almond flour
- 60 millilitres (¼ cup) water
- 55 grams (½ cup) low-fat feta cheese, crumbled
- 2 green onions (scallions), chopped
- Ground black pepper, as required

Directions:

1. In a bowl, whisk the egg whites well.
2. Add the almond flour, baking powder, and water and beat until smooth.
3. Add the feta cheese, spinach, green onions (scallions), garlic, nutmeg, salt and black pepper and stir to combine.
4. Heat a greased non-stick wok over medium heat.
5. Add desired amount of the mixture and tilt the pan to spread it in an even layer.
6. Cook for about 3-4 minutes or until golden brown.
7. Flip the side and cook for about 2-3 more minutes.
8. Repeat with the remaining mixture.
9. Serve warm.

Vanilla Waffles

Servings|2   Time|20 minutes
Nutritional Content (per serving):
Cal| 87   Fat| 0.9g   Protein| 10.4g   Carbs| 8g   Fibre| 0.8g

Ingredients:

- ❖ 25 grams (¼ cup) coconut flour
- ❖ 60 millilitres (¼ cup) unsweetened almond milk
- ❖ 1¼ millilitres (¼ teaspoon) organic vanilla extract
- ❖ 6 egg whites
- ❖ 4 grams (1 teaspoon) baking powder
- ❖ 15 grams (1 tablespoon) maple syrup

Directions:

1. Preheat the waffle iron and lightly grease it.
2. In a large bowl, add the flour and baking powder and mix well.
3. Add the remaining ingredients and mix until well combined.
4. Place half of the mixture in the preheated waffle iron.
5. Cook for about 3-5 minutes or until waffles become golden brown.
6. Repeat with the remaining mixture.
7. Serve warm.

Cinnamon Waffles

Servings|2 Time|20 minutes
Nutritional Content (per serving):
Cal| 29   Fat| 06g   Protein| 3.9g   Carbs| 2.3g   Fibre| 1.2g

Ingredients:

- 2 egg whites
- 1 gram (¼ teaspoon) baking powder
- 45 millilitres (3 tablespoons) unsweetened almond milk
- 15 grams (2 tablespoons) coconut flour
- 2½ grams (½ teaspoon) ground cinnamon

Directions:

1. Preheat the waffle iron and then grease it.
2. In a medium-sized bowl, add all ingredients and mix until well combined.
3. Place half of the mixture into the preheated waffle iron and cook for about 3-5 minutes or until golden brown.
4. Repeat with the remaining mixture.
5. Serve warm.

Blueberry Muffins

Servings|10   Time|22 minutes
Nutritional Content (per serving):
Cal| 65   Fat| 3.1g   Protein| 2.2g   Carbs| 6.4g   Fibre| 2g

Ingredients:

- 50 grams (½ cup) gluten-free rolled oats
- 30 grams (2 tablespoons) flaxseeds
- Pinch of ground nutmeg
- 2 egg whites
- ¼ of banana, peeled
- 2½ millilitres (½ teaspoon) organic vanilla extract

- 25 grams (¼ cup) almond flour
- 2 grams (½ teaspoon) baking soda
- 2½ grams (½ teaspoon) ground cinnamon
- 60 grams (¼ cup) almond butter, softened
- 40 grams (¼ cup) fresh blueberries

Directions:

1. Preheat your oven to 190 °C (375 °F). Grease 10 cups of a muffin tin.
2. In a high-power blender, add all ingredients except for blueberries and pulse until smooth and creamy.
3. Transfer the mixture into a bowl and gently fold in blueberries.
4. Place the mixture into prepared muffin cups evenly.
5. Bake for approximately 10-12 minutes or until a toothpick inserted in the centre comes out clean.
6. Remove the muffin tin from oven and place onto a wire rack to cool for about 10 minutes.
7. Then invert the muffins onto the wire rack to cool completely before serving.

Chicken Muffins

Servings|8   Time|35 minutes
Nutritional Content (per serving):
Cal| 90   Fat| 1g   Protein| 15.8g   Carbs| 3.6g   Fibre| 0.6g

Ingredients:

- 16 egg whites
- 30 millilitres (2 tablespoons) water
- 150 grams (1 cup) capsicum (bell pepper), seeded and chopped

- Ground black pepper, as required
- 225 grams (8 ounces) cooked chicken, finely chopped
- 120 grams (1 cup) onion, chopped

Directions:

1. Preheat your oven to 180 °C (350 °F). Grease 8 cups of a muffin tin.
2. In a bowl, add egg whites, black pepper and water and beat until well combined.
3. Add chicken, bell pepper and onion and stir to combine.
4. Transfer the mixture in prepared muffin cups evenly.
5. Bake for approximately 18-20 minutes or until golden brown.
6. Remove the muffin tin from oven and place onto a wire rack to cool for about 10 minutes.
7. Then invert the muffins onto a platter and serve warm.

Veggie Muffins

Servings|12   Time|27 minutes
Nutritional Content (per serving):
Cal| 36   Fat| 1.3g   Protein| 4.7g   Carbs| 1.6g   Fibre| 0.5g

Ingredients:

- ❖ 45-60 millilitres (3-4 tablespoons) unsweetened almond milk
- ❖ 25 grams (½ cup) sun-dried tomatoes in oil, drained and chopped
- ❖ 45 grams (¼ cup) canned artichokes in oil, drained and sliced thinly
- ❖ 10 grams (¼ cup) fresh parsley, chopped
- ❖ 12 large egg whites
- ❖ Ground black pepper, as required
- ❖ 70 grams (1/3 cup) Kalamata olives, pitted and quartered
- ❖ 40 grams (¼ cup) capsicum (bell pepper), seeded and chopped
- ❖ 55 grams (½ cup) low-fat feta cheese, crumbled

Directions:

1. Preheat your oven to 190 °C (375 °F). Grease a 24 cups mini muffin tin.
2. In a bowl, add almond milk egg whites and black pepper and black pepper and beat well.
3. In another large bowl, mix together the vegetables.
4. Place the egg mixture into prepared muffin cups about ¾ of full.
5. Place vegetables mixture over egg mixture evenly and top with remaining egg mixture.
6. Sprinkle with feta and parsley evenly.
7. Bake for about 10-12 minutes or until eggs are done completely.
8. Remove the muffin tin from oven and place onto a wire rack to cool for about 5 minutes before serving.
9. Then invert the muffins onto a serving platter and serve warm.

Quinoa Bread

Servings|12   Time|2 hours
Nutritional Content (per serving):
Cal| 156   Fat| 6.5g   Protein| 4.6g   Carbs| 19.3g   Fibre| 3.1g

Ingredients:

- 335 grams (1¾ cups) uncooked quinoa
- Pinch of sea salt
- 15 millilitres (1 tablespoon) fresh lemon juice
- 40 grams (¼ cup) chia seeds
- 2 grams (½ teaspoon) bicarbonate soda
- 60 millilitres (¼ cup) olive oil
- 120 millilitres (½ cup) water

Directions:

1. In a large bowl of water, soak the quinoa overnight.
2. In another bowl, soak the chia seeds in 120 millilitres (½ cup) of water overnight.
3. Drain the quinoa and rinse well.
4. Again, drain the quinoa completely.
5. Preheat your oven to 160 °C (320 °F). Line a loaf pan with parchment paper.
6. Add all the ingredients in a food processor and pulse for about 3 minutes.
7. Place the mixture into the prepared loaf pan evenly.
8. Bake for about 1½ hours or until a toothpick inserted in the center comes out clean.
9. Remove from the oven and place the loaf pan onto a wire rack to cool for at least 10-15 minutes.
10. Then invert the bread onto the rack to cool completely before slicing.
11. Cut the bread loaf into desired-sized slices and serve.

Blueberry Bread

Servings|16   Time|38 minutes
Nutritional Content (per serving):
Cal| 131   Fat| 4.5g   Protein| 1.9g   Carbs| 21.6g   Fibre| 2g

Ingredients:

- 180 grams (2 cups) gluten-free oat flour
- 3 grams (¾ teaspoon) baking powder
- 150 grams (½ cup) maple syrup
- 60 millilitres (¼ cup) unsweetened almond milk
- 75 grams (½ cup) fresh blueberries
- 4 grams (1 teaspoon) baking soda
- Pinch of sea salt
- 450 grams (1½ cups) overripe bananas, peeled and mashed
- 60 millilitres (¼ cup) olive oil
- 10 millilitres (2 teaspoons) organic vanilla extract

Directions:

1. Preheat your oven to 180 ºC (350 ºF). Arrange a rack in the centre of oven.
2. Grease a loaf pan.
3. In a large bowl, blend together the flour, baking soda, baking powder and salt.
4. In another bowl, add the remaining ingredients except for blueberries and whisk until well combined.
5. Add the flour mixture and mix until just combined.
6. Gently fold in the blueberries.
7. Place the mixture into the prepared loaf pan evenly.
8. Bake for about 38 minutes or until a toothpick inserted in the centre comes out clean.
9. Switch off the oven but keep the loaf pan inside for about 10-15 minutes.
10. Remove from the oven and place the loaf pan onto a wire rack to cool for at least 10-15 minutes.
11. Then invert the bread onto the rack to cool completely before slicing.
12. Cut the bread loaf into desired-sized slices and serve.

Courgette Bread

Servings|6   Time|1 hour
Nutritional Content (per serving):
Cal| 132   Fat| 5.3g   Protein| 3.2g   Carbs| 20.5g   Fibre| 3.4g

Ingredients:

- 50 grams (½ cup) almond flour, sifted
- 2½ grams (½ teaspoon) ground cinnamon
- 450 grams (1½ cups) banana, peeled and mashed
- 8 grams (2 teaspoons) organic vanilla extract
- 6 grams (1½ teaspoons) baking soda
- 1¼ grams (¼ teaspoon) ground cardamom
- 60 grams (¼ cup) almond butter, softened
- 115 grams (1 cup) courgette (zucchini), shredded

Directions:

1. Preheat your oven to 180 ºC (350 ºF). Grease a loaf pan.
2. In a large bowl, mix together the flour, baking soda and spices.
3. In another bowl, add the remaining ingredients except zucchini and beat until well combined.
4. Fold in the grated courgette (zucchini).
5. Transfer the batter into the prepared loaf pan.
6. Bake for about 40-45 minutes or until a toothpick inserted in the centre comes out clean.
7. Remove from oven and place the loaf pan onto a wire rack to cool for at least 10 minutes.
8. Then invert the bread onto the rack to cool completely before slicing.
9. Cut the bread loaf into desired-sized slices and serve.

Blueberry Toasts

Servings|2   Time|10 minutes
Nutritional Content (per serving):
Cal| 196   Fat| 7.3g   Protein| 9.4g   Carbs| 23.5g   Fibre| 2.7g

Ingredients:

- 2 whole-wheat bread slices
- 40 grams (¼ cup) fresh blueberries
- 15 grams (2 teaspoons) honey
- 110 grams (½ cup) part-skim ricotta cheese
- 10 grams (1 tablespoon) unsalted almonds, chopped

Directions:

1. Arrange the bread slices onto serving plates.
2. Top each slice with ricotta, followed by blueberries and almonds.
3. Drizzle with honey and serve.

Lunch Recipes

Apple & Strawberry Salad

Servings|4   Time|15 minutes
Nutritional Content (per serving):
Cal| 200   Fat| 10.3g   Protein| 1.6g   Carbs| 23.3g   Fibre| 4.5g

Ingredients:

For Salad:

- ❖ 300 grams (4 cups) lettuce, torn
- ❖ 2 apples, cored and sliced
- ❖ 105 grams (1 cup) fresh strawberries, hulled and sliced
- ❖ 30 grams (¼ cup) unsalted pecans, chopped

For Dressing:

- ❖ 30 millilitres (2 tablespoons) apple cider vinegar
- ❖ 30 millilitres (2 tablespoons) olive oil
- ❖ 15 grams (1 tablespoon) maple syrup

Directions:

1. For salad: place all the ingredients in a large bowl and mix well.
2. For dressing: place all the ingredients in a bowl and beat until well combined.
3. Pour the dressing over the salad and toss it all to coat well.
4. Serve immediately.

Raspberry Salad

Servings|3   Time|10 minutes
Nutritional Content (per serving):
Cal| 131   Fat| 9.3g   Protein| 2.5g   Carbs| 8.2g   Fibre| 3.7g

Ingredients:

For Salad:

- ❖ 60 grams (3 cups) fresh baby arugula
- ❖ 125 grams (1 cup) fresh raspberries
- ❖ 5 grams (1 tablespoon) fresh mint leaves, finely chopped
- ❖ 25 grams (¼ cup) unsalted walnuts, chopped

For Dressing:

- ❖ 15 millilitres (1 tablespoon) olive oil
- ❖ 15 millilitres (1 tablespoon) fresh lime juice
- ❖ 5 grams (1 teaspoon) maple syrup
- ❖ Pinch of sea salt

Directions:

1. For salad: place all ingredients in a salad bowl and mix.
2. For dressing: place all ingredients in another bowl and beat until well combined.
3. Pour the dressing over salad and toss to coat well.
4. Serve immediately.

Beet Salad

Servings|4   Time|1¼ hours
Nutritional Content (per serving):
Cal| 118   Fat| 8.2g   Protein| 3.2g   Carbs| 10.3g   Fibre| 2.6g

Ingredients:

- 3 medium beets, trimmed
- 15 millilitres (1 tablespoon) balsamic vinegar
- Ground black pepper, as required
- 25 grams (¼ cup) unsalted walnuts, chopped
- 15 millilitres (1 tablespoon) olive oil
- 5 grams (1 teaspoon) maple syrup
- Pinch of sea salt
- 120 grams (4 cups) fresh spinach, torn

Directions:

1. Preheat your oven to 200 °C (400 °F).
2. With a piece foil, wrap each beet completely.
3. Arrange the foil packets onto a baking sheet and roast for about 1 hour.
4. Remove from the oven and carefully open the foil packets.
5. Set aside to cool slightly.
6. With a paper towel, remove the peel of beets and then cut them into chunks.
7. In a serving bowl, add the oil, vinegar, maple syrup, salt and black pepper and beat well.
8. Add beet chunks, spinach and walnuts and toss to coat well.
9. Serve immediately.

Courgette & Tomato Salad

Servings|4   Time|15 minutes
Nutritional Content (per serving):
Cal| 95   Fat| 6.3g   Protein| 2.1g   Carbs| 7.3g   Fibre| 2.3g

Ingredients:

- ❖ 2 medium courgettes (zucchinis), sliced thinly
- ❖ 30 millilitres (2 tablespoons) olive oil
- ❖ Pinch of sea salt
- ❖ 400 grams (2 cups) tomatoes, sliced
- ❖ 30 millilitres (2 tablespoons) fresh lime juice

Directions:

1. In a salad bowl, place all ingredients and gently toss to combine.
2. Serve immediately.

Shrimp Lettuce Wraps

Servings|5   Time|20 minutes
Nutritional Content (per serving):
Cal| 172   Fat| 3.3g   Protein| 30.4g   Carbs| 2.6g   Fibre| 0.1g

Ingredients:

- ❖ 5 millilitres (1 teaspoon) olive oil
- ❖ Pinch of sea salt
- ❖ 1 garlic clove, minced
- ❖ 10 large lettuce leaves

- ❖ 680 grams (1½ pounds) shrimp, peeled, deveined and chopped
- ❖ 5 grams (2 tablespoons) fresh chives, minced

Directions:

1. In a large wok, heat the olive oil over medium heat and sauté garlic for about 1 minute.
2. Add the shrimp and cook for about 3-4 minutes.
3. Remove from heat and set aside to cool slightly.
4. Arrange lettuce leaves onto serving plates.
5. Divide the shrimp over the leaves evenly.
6. Garnish with chives and serve immediately.

Tofu Lettuce Wraps

Servings|4   Time|26 minutes
Nutritional Content (per serving):
Cal| 136   Fat| 8.3g   Protein| 10.2g   Carbs| 5.5g   Fibre| 1.5g

Ingredients:

- 15 millilitres (1 tablespoon) olive oil
- 5 grams (1 teaspoon) curry powder
- 8 lettuce leaves
- 5 grams (2 tablespoons) fresh coriander (cilantro), chopped
- 395 grams (14 ounces) extra-firm tofu, drained, pressed and cut into cubes
- Pinch of sea salt
- 2 small carrots, peeled and julienned

Directions:

1. In a wok, heat the oil over medium heat and cook the tofu, curry powder and a little salt for about 5-6 minutes or until golden brown, stirring frequently.
2. Remove from the heat and set aside to cool slightly.
3. Arrange the lettuce leaves onto serving plates.
4. Divide the tofu and carrot over each leaf evenly.
5. Garnish with coriander (cilantro) and serve.

Stuffed Sweet Potato

Servings|2   Time|55 minutes
Nutritional Content (per serving):
Cal| 312   Fat| 13.3g   Protein| 6.3g   Carbs| 37.6g   Fibre| 6.4g

Ingredients:

- ❖ 1 large sweet potato, halved
- ❖ 60 grams (1/3 cup) cooked chickpeas
- ❖ 70 grams (1/3 cup) cooked quinoa
- ❖ 1¼ grams (¼ teaspoon) paprika
- ❖ 5 grams (1 tablespoon) fresh coriander (cilantro), chopped
- ❖ 30 millilitres (2 tablespoons) olive oil, divided
- ❖ 5 grams (1 teaspoon) curry powder
- ❖ Ground black pepper, as required
- ❖ 5 millilitres (1 teaspoon) fresh lime juice

Directions:

1. Preheat your oven to 190 °C (375 °F).
2. Rub each sweet potato half with half of oil evenly.
3. Arrange the sweet potato halves onto a baking sheet, cut side down.
4. Bake for 40 minutes or until sweet potato becomes tender.
5. Meanwhile, for filling: in a wok, heat the remaining oil over medium heat and cook the chickpeas, curry powder and paprika for about 6-8 minutes, stirring frequently.
6. Stir in the cooked quinoa and black pepper and remove from the heat.
7. Remove from the oven and arrange each sweet potato halves onto a plate.
8. With a fork, fluff the flesh of each half slightly.
9. Place chickpeas mixture in each half and drizzle with lime juice
10. Serve immediately with the garnishing of coriander (cilantro).

Turkey Burgers

Servings|8   Time|36 minutes
Nutritional Content (per serving):
Cal| 147   Fat| 8.3g   Protein| 12.4g   Carbs| 4g   Fibre| 1.4g

Ingredients:

- 455 grams (1 pound) lean ground turkey
- 1 medium beet, trimmed, peeled and finely chopped
- 5 grams (1 tablespoon) fresh coriander (cilantro), finely chopped
- Ground black pepper, as required
- 240 grams (8 cups) fresh baby spinach
- 1 carrot, peeled and finely chopped
- 1 small onion, finely chopped
- 2 Serrano peppers, seeded and chopped
- Pinch of sea salt
- 45 millilitres (3 tablespoons) olive oil

Directions:

1. In a large bowl, add all ingredients except for oil and mix until well combined.
2. Make 8 equal-sized patties from mixture.
3. In a large non-stick wok, heat the olive oil over medium heat and cook the patties in 2 batches for about 3-4 minutes per side or until golden brown.
4. Serve alongside the spinach.

Beans & Quinoa Burgers

Servings|4   Time|1 hour 20 minutes
Nutritional Content (per serving):

Cal| 293   Fat| 4.3g   Protein| 13.4g   Carbs| 51.6g   Fibre| 12.7g

Ingredients:

- 95 grams (½ cup) uncooked quinoa, rinsed
- 15 grams (1 tablespoon) flaxseeds meal
- 340 grams (2 cups) cooked black beans
- 35 grams (1/3 cup) gluten-free oat flour
- 60 grams (½ cup) onion, finely chopped
- Pinch of sea salt
- Ground black pepper, as required
- 240 millilitres (1 cup) plus 45 millilitres (3 tablespoons) water, divided
- 5 grams (1 teaspoon) dried thyme
- 65 grams (½ cup) fresh corn
- 75 grams (½ cup) capsicum (bell pepper), seeded and finely chopped
- 30 millilitres (2 tablespoons) fresh lemon juice

Directions:

1. Preheat your oven to 190 °C (375 °F). Line a baking sheet with greased parchment paper.
2. For patties: in a medium saucepan, add 240 millilitres (1 cup) of water and quinoa over medium-high heat and bring to a boil.
3. Adjust the heat to low and simmer, covered for about 15 minutes.
4. Remove from the heat and set aside, covered for about 5-10 minutes.
5. In a small bowl, add the remaining water and flaxseed and mix well. Set aside for about 5 minutes.
6. In a large bowl, add ¾ of the beans and with a fork, mash them.
7. Add the remaining beans, flaxseed mixture, quinoa and remaining ingredients except for spinach and mix until well combined.
8. Make equal-sized patties from the mixture.
9. Arrange the patties onto the prepared baking sheet in a single layer.
10. Bake for approximately 15 minutes per side.
11. Serve immediately alongside the spinach.

Lentil Burgers

Servings|4   Time|1 hour 20 minutes
Nutritional Content (per serving):
Cal| 106   Fat| 2.8g   Protein| 6.4g   Carbs| 15.5g   Fibre| 6g

Ingredients:

- 420 millilitres (1¾ cups) plus 45 millilitres (3 tablespoons) water, divided
- 1 onion, chopped
- 15 grams (1 tablespoon) flaxseeds meal
- 2½ grams (½ teaspoon) ground cumin
- Ground black pepper, as required
- Olive oil cooking spray
- 210 grams (1 cup) dry lentils, rinsed
- 5 millilitres (1 teaspoon) olive oil
- 1 garlic clove, pressed
- 5 grams (2 tablespoons) fresh parsley, chopped
- Pinch of sea salt
- 80 grams (4 cups) fresh baby arugula

Directions:

1. In a saucepan, add 1¾ cups of water and lentils over medium-high heat and bring to a boil.
2. Adjust the heat to low and cook for about 15-20 minutes.
3. Preheat your oven to 195 °C (390 °F). Line a baking sheet with greased parchment paper.
4. In a small bowl, add the remaining water and flaxseed and mix well. Set aside for about 5 minutes.
5. In a wok, heat the oil over medium heat and sauté onion for about 5 minutes.
6. Remove from the heat and transfer into a bowl.
7. In the bowl of cooked onions, add the lentils, flaxseed mixture and remaining ingredients and mix until well combined.
8. Set the mixture aside to cool slightly.
9. With moistened hands, make the patties from the mixture.
10. Arrange the patties onto the prepared baking sheet in a single layer and spray with cooking spray.
11. Bake for approximately 20-25 minutes.
12. Serve hot alongside the arugula.

Turkey Meatballs

Servings|4   Time|30 minutes
Nutritional Content (per serving):
Cal| 279   Fat| 15.3g   Protein| 26.4g   Carbs| 6.9g   Fibre| 1.3g

Ingredients:

- 455 grams (1 pound) lean ground turkey
- 55 grams (½ cup) low-fat feta cheese, crumbled
- 30 millilitres (2 tablespoons) olive oil
- 220 grams (4 cups) fresh baby kale
- 30 grams (1 cup) frozen chopped spinach, thawed and squeezed
- 2½ grams (½ teaspoon) dried oregano
- Pinch of sea salt
- Ground black pepper, as required

Directions:

1. Place all ingredients except for oil and kale in a bowl and mix until well combined.
2. Make 12 equal-sized meatballs form the mixture.
3. Heat the olive oil in a large non-stick wok over medium heat and cook the meatballs for about 10-15 minutes or until done completely, flipping occasionally.
4. Serve alongside the kale.

Beans & Oat Falafel

Servings|4   Time|40 minutes
Nutritional Content (per serving):
Cal| 280   Fat| 8.3g   Protein| 14.4g   Carbs| 38.6g   Fibre| 11.7g

Ingredients:

- 60 grams (½ cup) unsalted pumpkin seeds
- 10 grams (2 teaspoons) dried oregano
- 5 grams (1 teaspoon) ground cumin
- 340 grams (2 cups) cooked black beans
- 30 millilitres (2 tablespoons) fresh lime juice
- 80 grams (4 cups) fresh baby arugula
- 50 grams (½ cup) gluten-free oats
- 5 grams (1 teaspoon) ground coriander
- 5 grams (1 teaspoon) red chili powder
- 40 grams (2 tablespoons) homemade tomato paste
- 10 grams (1 tablespoon) whole-wheat flour

Directions:

1. Preheat your oven to 180 °C (350 °F). Line a baking sheet with greased parchment paper.
2. In a food processor, add the pumpkin seeds, oats, oregano and spices and pulse until oats are broken down.
3. Add the black beans, tomato paste, lime juice and flour and mix until well combined.
4. Make equal-sized balls from the mixture.
5. Arrange the balls onto the prepared baking sheet in a single layer and gently press each slightly.
6. Bake for approximately 20 minutes.
7. Serve hot alongside the arugula.

Chickpeas Falafel

Servings|4   Time|55 minutes
Nutritional Content (per serving):
Cal| 141   Fat| 5.3g   Protein| 5.6g   Carbs| 19.6g   Fibre| 5.1g

Ingredients:

- 210 grams (1 cup) dried chickpeas, rinsed
- 4 garlic cloves, peeled
- 15 grams (½ cup) fresh parsley
- 15 millilitres (1 tablespoon) olive oil
- Pinch of sea salt
- 300 grams (4 cups) lettuce, torn
- 60 grams (½ cup) onion, roughly chopped
- 15 grams (½ cup) fresh coriander (cilantro)
- 2½ grams (½ teaspoon) ground cumin
- Ground black pepper, as required

Directions:

1. In a large bowl of water, place the chickpeas and refrigerate for 12-24 hours.
2. Then drain the chickpeas.
3. Preheat your oven to 190 °C (375 °F). Place a rack in the middle of the oven. Generously, grease a large rimmed baking sheet.
4. For falafel: in a food processor, add all the ingredients and pulse until smooth.
5. Take about 2 tablespoons of the mixture and shape it into a 1¼-centimetre (½-inch) thick patty.
6. Repeat with the remaining mixture.
7. Arrange the patties onto the prepared baking sheet in a single layer.
8. Bake for about 25-30 minutes, flipping once halfway through.
9. Serve hot alongside the lettuce.

Lentil Falafel

Servings|4   Time|35 minutes
Nutritional Content (per serving):
Cal| 275   Fat| 6.3g   Protein| 15.1g   Carbs| 36.9g   Fibre| 5.5g

Ingredients:

- 10 grams (¼ cup) fresh parsley
- 2 garlic cloves, peeled
- 15 grams (2 tablespoons) chickpea flour
- 30 millilitres (2 tablespoons) olive oil
- Pinch of sea salt
- Ground black pepper, as required
- 1 small red onion, roughly chopped
- 210 grams (1 cup) lentils, soaked overnight
- 30 millilitres (2 tablespoons) fresh lemon juice
- 2½ grams (½ teaspoon) ground cumin
- 120 grams (4 cups) fresh baby spinach

Directions:

1. Preheat your oven to 200 ºC (400 ºF). Line a baking sheet with parchment paper.
2. In a food processor, add the parsley, onion and garlic and pulse until finely chopped.
3. Now, place the remaining ingredients and pulse until just combined.
4. Make small equal-sized patties from the mixture.
5. Arrange the patties onto the prepared baking sheet in a single layer.
6. Bake for about 18-20 minutes or until patties become golden brown.
7. Serve hot alongside the spinach.

Broccoli & Spinach Soup

Servings|4   Time|35 minutes
Nutritional Content (per serving):
Cal| 142   Fat| 7.3g   Protein| 7.4g   Carbs| 13g   Fibre| 5.4g

Ingredients:

- 15 millilitres (1 tablespoon) olive oil
- 3-4 garlic cloves, chopped
- 2 celery stalks, chopped
- 1-2 green chilies, chopped
- 720 millilitres (3 cups) salt-free vegetable broth
- 120 grams (4 cups) fresh spinach, torn
- 10 millilitres (2 teaspoons) fresh lemon juice
- 60 grams (½ cup) onion, chopped
- 270 grams (3 cups) broccoli, cut into small pieces
- 1 carrot, peeled and chopped
- Pinch of sea salt
- 360 millilitres (1½ cups) unsweetened almond milk
- 20 grams (2 tablespoons) chia seeds
- Ground black pepper, as required

Directions:

1. Heat olive oil in a saucepan over medium heat and sauté the onion and garlic for about 4-5 minutes.
2. Add the broccoli, celery, carrot, green chilies, salt, broth and almond milk and bring to a boil.
3. Now, adjust the heat to medium-low and cook for about 10 minutes.
4. Add spinach and chia seeds and cook for about 1-2 minutes.
5. Remove the pan of soup from heat and with an immersion blender, blend until smooth.
6. Drizzle with lemon juice and serve hot.

Squash & Apple Soup

Servings|4   Time|1 hour
Nutritional Content (per serving):
Cal| 208   Fat| 7.3g   Protein| 2.4g   Carbs| 37.9g   Fibre| 7g

Ingredients:

- 30 millilitres (2 tablespoons) olive oil
- 2 garlic cloves, minced
- 630 grams (3 cups) butternut squash, peeled, seeded and cubed
- 960 millilitres (4 cups) water
- Pinch of sea salt
- 120 grams (1 cup) onion, chopped
- 5 grams (1 teaspoon) dried thyme
- 2 apples, peeled, cored and chopped
- Ground black pepper, as required

Directions:

1. In a soup pan, heat olive oil over medium heat and sauté the onion for about 5 minutes.
2. Add the garlic and thyme and sauté for about 1 minute.
3. Add the squash and apple and ginger and cook for about 1-2 minutes.
4. Stir in the water and bring to a boil.
5. Now, adjust the heat to low and simmer covered for about 30 minutes.
6. Stir in the salt and black pepper and remove from the heat.
7. With a hand blender, puree the soup mixture until smooth.
8. Serve immediately.

Cauliflower with Green Peas

Servings|3   Time|30 minutes
Nutritional Content (per serving):
Cal| 182   Fat| 9.3g   Protein| 5.8g   Carbs| 19.3g   Fibre| 6.5g

Ingredients:

- 2 medium tomatoes, chopped
- 30 millilitres (2 tablespoons) olive oil
- 5 grams (1 teaspoon) ground cumin
- 5 grams (1 teaspoon) cayenne pepper
- 1¼ grams (¼ teaspoon) ground turmeric
- 145 grams (1 cup) fresh green peas, shelled
- 120 millilitres (½ cup) warm water

- 60 millilitres (¼ cup) water
- 3 garlic cloves, minced
- 10 grams (2 teaspoons) fresh ginger, minced
- 5 grams (1 teaspoon) ground coriander
- 210 grams (2 cups) cauliflower, chopped
- Pinch of sea salt
- Ground black pepper, as required

Directions:

1. In a high-power blender, add tomato and 60 millilitres (¼ cup) of water and pulse until smooth puree forms. Set aside.
2. In a large wok, heat the oil over medium heat and sauté the garlic, ginger, green chilies and spices for about 1 minute.
3. Add the cauliflower, peas and tomato puree and cook, stirring for about 3-4 minutes.
4. Add the warm water and bring to a boil.
5. Reduce the heat to medium-low and cook, covered for about 8-10 minutes or until vegetables are done completely.
6. Serve hot.

Tofu with Green Peas

Servings|6   Time|35 minutes
Nutritional Content (per serving):
Cal| 242   Fat| 9.3g   Protein| 15.4g   Carbs| 24.9g   Fibre| 7.9g

Ingredients:

- ❖ 30 millilitres (2 tablespoons) olive oil, divided
- ❖ 120 grams (1 cup) onion, chopped
- ❖ 2 garlic cloves, minced
- ❖ 2 large tomatoes, finely chopped
- ❖ 60 millilitres (¼ cup) water
- ❖ 510 grams (18 ounces) extra-firm tofu, pressed, drained and cubed
- ❖ 10 grams (2 teaspoons) fresh ginger, minced
- ❖ 725 grams (5 cups) frozen green peas, thawed

Directions:

1. In a large wok, heat half of oil over medium-high heat and cook the tofu for about 4-5 minutes or until browned completely, stirring occasionally.
2. Transfer the tofu into a bowl
3. In the same wok, heat the remaining oil over medium heat and sauté the onion for about 3-4 minutes.
4. Add the ginger and garlic and sauté for about 1 minute.
5. Add the tomatoes and cook for about 4-5 minutes, crushing with the back of the spoon.
6. Stir in all the peas and water and cook for about 3-5 minutes.
7. Serve hot.

Tofu with Brussels Sprout

Servings|4   Time|30 minutes
Nutritional Content (per serving):
Cal| 278   Fat| 14.3g   Protein| 12.4g   Carbs| 19.2g   Fibre| 7g

Ingredients:

- ❖ 30 millilitres (2 tablespoons) olive oil, divided
- ❖ 2 garlic cloves, chopped
- ❖ 45 grams (1/3 cup) unsalted pecans, chopped
- ❖ 570 grams (1¼ pounds) Brussels sprout, trimmed and cut into wide ribbons
- ❖ 285 grams (10 ounces) extra-firm tofu, pressed, drained and cut into slices
- ❖ 15 grams (1 tablespoon) maple syrup
- ❖ 15 grams (¼ cup) fresh coriander (cilantro), chopped

Directions:

1. In a wok, heat half of the oil over medium heat and sauté the tofu and for about 6-7 minutes or until golden brown.
2. Add the garlic and pecans and sauté for about 1 minute.
3. Add the applesauce and cook for about 2 minutes.
4. Stir in the coriander (cilantro) and remove from heat.
5. Transfer tofu into a plate and set aside
6. In the same wok, heat the remaining oil over medium-high heat and cook the Brussels sprouts for about 5 minutes.
7. Stir in the tofu and remove from the heat.
8. Serve immediately.

Quinoa with Green Peas

Servings|5   Time|22 minutes
Nutritional Content (per serving):
Cal| 348   Fat| 8.3g   Protein| 12.4g   Carbs| 52.6g   Fibre| 9g

Ingredients:

- 30 millilitres (2 tablespoons) olive oil
- 555 grams (3 cups) cooked quinoa
- 25 grams (¼ cup) green onions (scallions), chopped
- 1 small onion, chopped
- 290 grams (2 cups) frozen green peas, thawed
- 60 millilitres (¼ cup tablespoons) salt-free vegetable broth

Directions:

1. In a large wok, heat the oil over medium heat.
2. Add the onion and sauté for about 4-5 minutes.
3. Add the peas and cook for about 3-4 minutes.
4. Stir in the remaining ingredients and cook for about 2-3 minutes or until heated through.
5. Serve hot.

Quinoa with Mushroom

Servings|4   Time|45 minutes
Nutritional Content (per serving):
Cal| 219   Fat| 5.3g   Protein| 9.4g   Carbs| 34.3g   Fibre| 4.4g

Ingredients:

- 10 millilitres (2 teaspoons) olive oil
- 340 grams (12 ounces) fresh mushrooms, sliced
- 15 grams (¼ cup) fresh coriander (cilantro), chopped
- Pinch of sea salt

- 190 grams (1 cup) uncooked quinoa, rinsed
- 3 garlic cloves, minced
- 420 millilitres (1¾ cups) water
- 1¼ grams (¼ teaspoon) cayenne pepper

Directions:

1. In a medium saucepan, heat olive oil over medium-high heat and sauté the garlic for about 30-40 seconds.
2. Add the mushrooms and cook on for about 5-6 minutes, stirring frequently.
3. Stir in the quinoa and cook for about 2 minutes, stirring continuously.
4. Add the water, cayenne and salt and bring to a boil.
5. Now, adjust the heat to low and simmer, covered for about 15-18 minutes or until almost all the liquid is absorbed.
6. Serve hot with the garnishing of coriander (cilantro).

Dinner Recipes

Turkey & Lentil Soup

Servings|8   Time|2 hours
Nutritional Content (per serving):
Cal| 225   Fat| 5.1g   Protein| 16.8g   Carbs| 29.6g   Fibre| 8.2g

Ingredients:

- 30 millilitres (2 tablespoons) olive oil
- Pinch of sea salt
- 1 large carrot, peeled and chopped
- 5 grams (1 teaspoon) dried rosemary
- 2 large potatoes, peeled and chopped
- 420 grams (2 cups) dry lentils, rinsed
- 10 grams (¼ cup) fresh parsley, chopped
- 455 grams (1 pound) boneless, skinless turkey breast, cubed
- Ground black pepper, as required
- 1 celery stalk, chopped
- 1 large onion, chopped
- 6 garlic cloves, chopped
- 5 grams (1 teaspoon) dried oregano
- 1920 millilitres (8 cups) water
- 800 grams (4 cups) tomatoes, chopped

Directions:

1. Season the turkey cubes with salt and black pepper evenly.
2. In a large soup pan, heat the olive oil over medium-high heat and cook the turkey cubes for about 4-5 minutes or until browned from all sides.
3. With a slotted spoon, transfer the turkey cubes into a bowl and set aside.
4. In the same pan, add the carrot, celery onion, garlic and dried herbs over medium heat and cook for about 5 minutes.
5. Add potatoes and cook for about 4-5 minutes.
6. Add cooked turkey, tomatoes and water and bring to a boil over high heat.
7. Adjust the heat to low and cook, covered for about 1 hour.
8. Add the lentils and cook, covered for about 40 minutes.
9. Stir in black pepper and serve hot with the topping of parsley.

White Beans & Kale Soup

Servings|4   Time|1 hour 5 minutes
Nutritional Content (per serving):
Cal| 264   Fat| 3g   Protein| 12.4g   Carbs| 49.1g   Fibre| 10.2g

Ingredients:

- 10 millilitres (2 teaspoons) olive oil
- 5 grams (1 tablespoon) fresh rosemary leaves, minced
- Ground black pepper, as required
- 165 grams (3 cups) fresh kale, tough ribs removed and roughly chopped
- 1 medium onion, chopped
- 4 garlic cloves, minced
- 455 grams (1 pound) potatoes, peeled and cut into small cubes
- 960 millilitres (4 cups) water
- Pinch of sea salt
- 360 grams (2 cups) cooked white beans

Directions:

1. In a large saucepan, heat the oil over medium heat and cook the onions for about 7-9 minutes, stirring frequently.
2. Add the garlic and rosemary and sauté for about 1 minute.
3. Add the potatoes, water, salt and black pepper and bring to a boil.
4. Adjust the heat to low and simmer, uncovered for about 30-35 minutes.
5. With the back of a spoon, mash some of the potatoes roughly.
6. Stir in the beans and kale and simmer for about 4-7 minutes.
7. Serve hot.

Mixed Beans Soup

Servings|12   Time|1 hour 5 minutes
Nutritional Content (per serving):
Cal| 336   Fat| 66.g   Protein| 17g   Carbs| 55.9g   Fibre| 18.1g

Ingredients:

- 60 millilitres (¼ cup) olive oil
- 1 large sweet potato, peeled and cubed
- 4 garlic cloves, minced
- 1 (115-gram) (4-ounce) can green chilies
- 10 grams (1 tablespoon) ground cumin
- 850 grams (5 cups) cooked Great Northern beans
- 340 grams (2 cups) cooked black beans

- 30 grams (1 cup) fresh coriander (cilantro), chopped
- 1 large onion, chopped
- 3 carrots, peeled and chopped
- 3 celery stalks, chopped
- 10 grams (2 teaspoons) dried thyme, crushed
- 2 jalapeño peppers, chopped
- 4 large tomatoes, finely chopped
- 850 grams (5 cups) cooked red kidney beans
- 2160 millilitres (9 cups) salt-free vegetable broth

Directions:

1. In a Dutch oven, heat the oil over medium heat and sauté the onion, sweet potato, carrot and celery for about 6-8 minutes.
2. Add the garlic, thyme, green chilies, jalapeño peppers and cumin and sauté for about 1 minute.
3. Add in the tomatoes and cook for about 2-3 minutes.
4. Add the beans and broth and bring to a boil over medium-high heat.
5. Cover the pan with lid and cook for about 25-30 minutes.
6. Stir in the coriander (cilantro) and remove from heat.
7. Serve hot.

Oregano Chicken Breasts

Servings|7   Time|34 minutes
Nutritional Content (per serving):
Cal| 249   Fat| 9.3g   Protein| 33.2g   Carbs| 0.9g   Fibre| 0.6g

Ingredients:

- 4 (200-gram) (7-ounce) boneless, skinless chicken breasts
- 5 grams (1 teaspoon) dried oregano
- Pinch of sea salt
- 15 millilitres (1 tablespoon) olive oil
- 5 grams (1 teaspoon) paprika
- Ground black pepper, as required

Directions:

1. Preheat your oven to 220 °C (425 °F). Line a baking dish with parchment paper.
2. With a meat mallet, pound each chicken breast slightly.
3. In a bowl, mix together oregano, paprika, salt and black pepper.
4. Add chicken breasts and coat with oil mixture generously.
5. Arrange the chicken breasts onto the prepared baking dish in a single layer.
6. Bake for approximately 16 minutes.
7. Now, set the oven to broiler.
8. Broil the chicken breasts for about 2-3 minutes.
9. Remove the baking dish from oven and place the chicken breasts onto a cutting board for about 5 minutes.
10. Cut each chicken breast into desired-sized slices and serve.

Stuffed Chicken Breasts

Servings|4   Time|40 minutes
Nutritional Content (per serving):
Cal| 192   Fat| 6.3g   Protein| 26.4g   Carbs| 4g   Fibre| 1.1g

Ingredients:

- 15 millilitres (1 tablespoon) olive oil
- ½ of small capsicum (bell pepper), seeded and sliced thinly
- 2½ grams (½ teaspoon) dried oregano
- 4 (115-gram) (4-ounce) skinless, boneless chicken breasts, butterflied and pounded
- 1 small onion, chopped
- 1 pepperoni pepper, seeded and sliced thinly
- 2-3 garlic cloves, minced
- 30 grams (1 cup) fresh spinach, trimmed and chopped
- Pinch of sea salt
- Ground black pepper, as required

Directions:

1. Preheat your oven to 180 ºC (350 ºF). Line a baking sheet with parchment paper.
2. In a saucepan, heat the olive oil over medium heat and sauté onion, capsicum (bell pepper) and pepperoni pepper for about 1 minute.
3. Add the garlic and spinach and cook for about 2-3 minutes or until just wilted.
4. Stir in oregano, salt and black pepper and remove the saucepan from heat.
5. Place the chicken mixture into the middle of each butterflied chicken breast.
6. Fold each chicken breast over filling to make a little pocket and secure with toothpicks.
7. Arrange the chicken breasts onto the prepared baking sheet.
8. Bake for approximately 18-20 minutes.
9. Serve warm.

Chicken with Broccoli

Servings|6   Time|30 minutes
Nutritional Content (per serving):
Cal| 153   Fat| 5.3g   Protein| 19.2g   Carbs| 6.1g   Fibre| 2.2g

Ingredients:

- 20 millilitres (4 teaspoons) olive oil, divided
- 5 grams (1 teaspoon) fresh ginger, minced
- 450 grams (5 cups) broccoli, cut into bite-sized pieces
- 455 grams (1 pound) skinless, boneless chicken tenders, cubed
- 2 garlic cloves, minced
- 2½ grams (½ teaspoon) red pepper flakes, crushed
- 60 millilitres (¼ cup) water

Directions:

1. In a large non-stick wok, heat 2 teaspoons of oil over high heat and cook chicken for about 6-8 minutes, stirring frequently.
2. Transfer the chicken into a bowl and set aside.
3. In the same wok, heat the remaining oil over medium heat and sauté ginger, garlic and red pepper flakes for about 1 minute.
4. Add water and broccoli and stir fry for about 2-3 minutes.
5. Stir in chicken and cook for about 2-3 minutes, stirring frequently.
6. Serve hot.

Chicken with Mushroom Sauce

Servings|4 · Time|35 minutes
Nutritional Content (per serving):
Cal| 225   Fat| 11.3g   Protein| 23.4g   Carbs| 5.6g   Fibre| 1.5g

Ingredients:

- 15 grams (2 tablespoons) almond flour
- 4 (85-gram) (3-ounce) skinless, boneless chicken breasts
- 6 garlic cloves, chopped
- 180 millilitres (¾ cup) salt-free chicken broth
- 1¼ grams (¼ teaspoon) dried thyme
- Pinch of sea salt
- Ground black pepper, as required
- 30 millilitres (2 tablespoons) olive oil
- 340 grams (¾ pound) fresh mushrooms, sliced
- 60 millilitres (¼ cup) balsamic vinegar
- 1 bay leaf

Directions:

1. In a bowl, mix together flour, salt and black pepper.
2. Coat chicken breasts with flour mixture evenly.
3. In a wok, heat the olive oil over medium-high heat and stir fry chicken for about 3 minutes.
4. Add garlic and flip the chicken breasts.
5. Spread mushrooms over chicken and cook for about 3 minutes, shaking the wok frequently.
6. Add broth, vinegar, bay leaf and thyme and stir to combine.
7. Adjust the heat to medium-low and simmer, covered for about 8-10 minutes, flipping chicken occasionally.
8. With a slotted spoon, transfer the chicken onto a warm serving platter and with a piece of foil, cover to keep warm.
9. Place the pan of sauce over medium-high heat and cook, uncovered for about 7 minutes.
10. Remove the pan from heat and discard the bay leaf.
11. Place mushroom sauce over chicken and serve hot.

Chicken with Capsicums

Servings|6   Time|35 minutes
Nutritional Content (per serving):
Cal| 216   Fat| 19.3g   Protein| 22.4g   Carbs| 7.8g   Fibre| 1.8g

Ingredients:

- 45 millilitres (3 tablespoons) olive oil, divided
- 2 onions, sliced
- 4 garlic cloves, minced
- 5 grams (1 teaspoon) dried oregano
- 60 millilitres (¼ cup) salt-free chicken broth
- 10 grams (¼ cup) fresh parsley, chopped
- 5 (115-gram) (4-ounce) skinless, boneless chicken breasts, cut into strips
- 2 large capsicums (bell peppers), seeded and sliced
- 5 grams (1 teaspoon) dried basil
- Pinch of sea salt
- Ground black pepper, as required

Directions:

1. In a large non-stick wok, heat 15 millilitres (1 tablespoon) of olive oil over medium heat and cook the chicken strips for about 4-5 minutes or until browned completely.
2. With a slotted spoon, transfer the chicken strips into a bowl.
3. In the same wok, heat remaining oil over medium heat and sauté onions and garlic for about 2-3 minutes.
4. Stir in capsicums (bell peppers), dried herbs and broth cook for about 2 minutes.
5. Add cooked chicken strips and stir to combine.
6. Adjust the heat to low and cook, covered for about 10 minutes.
7. Stir in parsley and black pepper and remove from the heat.

Chicken with Pears

Servings|4   Time|40 minutes
Nutritional Content (per serving):
Cal| 248   Fat| 9.3g   Protein| 20.4g   Carbs| 18.4g   Fibre| 10.4g

Ingredients:

- 240 millilitres (1 cup) salt-free chicken broth
- 5 grams (2 teaspoons) tapioca flour
- 4 garlic cloves, minced
- 4 (85-gram) (3-ounce) skinless, boneless chicken breasts
- Ground black pepper as required
- 30 millilitres (2 tablespoons) apple cider vinegar
- 30 millilitres (2 tablespoons) olive oil
- 5 grams (2 tablespoons) fresh basil minced
- Pinch of sea salt
- 2 pears, cored and sliced

Directions:

1. In a bowl, blend together the broth, vinegar, and tapioca flour. Set aside.
2. In a large-sized cast-iron wok, heat oil over medium-high heat and sauté garlic and basil for about 1 minute.
3. Add the chicken, salt, and black pepper and cook for about 12-15 minutes.
4. Transfer the chicken into a bowl.
5. In the same wok, add the pears and cook for about 4-5 minutes.
6. Add the broth mixture and bring to a boil.
7. Cook for about 1 minute.
8. Add the chicken and stir to combine.
9. Now adjust the heat to low and cook for about 3-4 minutes.
10. Serve hot.

Ground Turkey with Mushrooms

Servings|4   Time|40 minutes
Nutritional Content (per serving):
Cal| 247   Fat| 14.3g   Protein| 23.4g   Carbs| 3.7g   Fibre| 0.9g

Ingredients:

- ❖ 455 grams (1 pound) lean ground turkey
- ❖ 2 garlic cloves, minced
- ❖ 200 grams (2 cups) fresh mushrooms, sliced
- ❖ 60 millilitres (¼ cup) salt-free chicken broth
- ❖ Pinch of sea salt
- ❖ 5 grams (2 tablespoons) fresh parsley, chopped
- ❖ 30 millilitres (2 tablespoons) olive oil
- ❖ ½ of onion, chopped
- ❖ 5 grams (2 tablespoons) fresh basil, chopped
- ❖ 30 millilitres (2 tablespoons) balsamic vinegar
- ❖ Ground black pepper, as required

Directions:

1. Heat a large non-stick wok over medium-high heat and cook the ground beef for about 8-10 minutes, breaking up the chunks with a wooden spoon.
2. With a slotted spoon, transfer the beef into a bowl.
3. In the same wok, add the onion and garlic for about 3 minutes.
4. Add the mushrooms and cook for about 5-7 minutes.
5. Add the cooked beef, basil, broth and vinegar and bring to a boil.
6. Adjust the heat to medium-low and simmer for about 3 minutes.
7. Stir in parsley and serve immediately.

Ground Turkey with Green Peas

Servings|4   Time|1 hour 5 minutes

Nutritional Content (per serving):
Cal| 251   Fat| 10.3g   Protein| 24.4g   Carbs| 11.2g   Fibre| 3.1g

Ingredients:

- 15 millilitres (1 tablespoon) olive oil
- 4 garlic cloves, minced
- 5 grams (1 teaspoon) ground coriander
- 2½ grams (½ teaspoon) ground turmeric
- 100 grams (½ cup) tomato, chopped
- 35 grams (2 tablespoons) fat-free plain Greek yoghurt, whipped
- Ground black pepper, as required
- 1 medium onion, chopped
- 1 (2½-centimetre) (1-inch) piece fresh ginger, minced
- 2½ grams (½ teaspoon) ground cumin
- 455 grams (1 pound) lean ground turkey
- 360 millilitres (1½ cups) water
- 145 grams (1 cup) fresh green peas, shelled
- 15 grams (¼ cup) fresh coriander (cilantro), chopped
- Pinch of sea salt

Directions:

1. In a Dutch oven, heat oil over medium-high heat and sauté the onion for about 3-4 minutes.
2. Add ginger, garlic, ground spices and bay leaf and sauté for about 1 minute.
3. Stir in turkey and cook for about 5 minutes.
4. Stir in tomato and cook for about 10 minutes, stirring occasionally.
5. Stir in water and green peas and bring to a gentle simmer.
6. Adjust the heat to low and cook, covered for about 25-30 minutes.
7. Stir in yoghurt, coriander (cilantro), salt and black pepper and cook for about 4-5 minutes.
8. Serve hot.

Parsley Salmon

Servings|6   Time|35 minutes
Nutritional Content (per serving):
Cal| 245   Fat| 14.3g   Protein| 22.4g   Carbs| 0.1g   Fibre| 0.1g

Ingredients:

- ❖ 6 (115-gram) (4-ounce) skinless salmon fillets
- ❖ Pinch of sea salt
- ❖ Ground black pepper, as required

- ❖ 30 millilitres (2 tablespoons) olive oil
- ❖ 10 grams (3 tablespoons) fresh parsley, minced

Directions:

1. Preheat your oven to 200 °C (400 °F). Grease a large baking dish.
2. In a bowl, place all ingredients and mix well.
3. Arrange the salmon fillets into the prepared baking dish in a single layer.
4. Bake for approximately 15-20 minutes or until desired doneness of salmon.
5. Serve hot.

Sweet & Sour Salmon

Servings|4   Time|35 minutes
Nutritional Content (per serving):
Cal| 229   Fat| 12.3g   Protein| 22.4g   Carbs| 3.5g   Fibre| 0.2g

Ingredients:

- ❖ 1 (2½-centimetre) (1-inch) piece fresh ginger, grated finely
- ❖ 20 grams (1 tablespoon) Dijon mustard
- ❖ 30 millilitres (2 tablespoons) olive oil
- ❖ 5 grams (2 tablespoons) fresh parsley, chopped
- ❖ 15 grams (1 tablespoon) honey
- ❖ 15 millilitres (1 tablespoon) fresh lemon juice
- ❖ 4 (115-gram) (4-ounce) salmon fillets

Directions:

1. In a bowl, mix together ginger, honey, lemon juice and Dijon mustard. Set aside.
2. In a large non-stick wok, heat olive oil over medium-high heat and cook the salmon fillets for about 3-4 minutes per side.
3. Stir in honey mixture and immediately remove from heat.
4. Serve hot.

Shrimp with Capsicums

Servings|4   Time|37 minutes
Nutritional Content (per serving):
Cal| 240   Fat| 8.3g   Protein| 26.4g   Carbs| 10.6g   Fibre| 1.8g

Ingredients:

- 30 millilitres (2 tablespoons) olive oil
- 455 grams (1 pound) medium shrimp, peeled and deveined
- 60 grams (½ cup) onion, sliced thinly
- 25 grams (¼ cup) green onion (scallion), chopped
- Ground black pepper, as required
- 4 garlic cloves, minced
- 1 fresh red chili pepper, sliced
- 300 grams (2 cups) capsicum (bell pepper), seeded and julienned
- 60 millilitres (¼ cup) salt-free chicken broth
- Pinch of sea salt

Directions:

1. In a large non-stick wok, heat olive oil over medium heat and sauté the garlic and red chili for about 2 minutes.
2. Add shrimp, capsicums (bell peppers), onion and black pepper and stir fry for about 5 minutes.
3. Stir in broth and cook for about 1 minute.
4. Stir in scallion and remove from the heat.
5. Serve hot.

Shrimp with Broccoli

Servings|4   Time|30 minutes
Nutritional Content (per serving):
Cal| 228   Fat| 8.3g   Protein| 27.4g   Carbs| 8.3g   Fibre| 2.2g

Ingredients:

- 30 millilitres (2 tablespoons) olive oil, divided
- ½ of onion, chopped
- 270 grams (3 cups) broccoli florets
- 5 grams (2 tablespoons) fresh parsley, chopped
- 455 grams (1 pound) large shrimp, peeled and deveined
- 3 garlic cloves, minced
- Pinch of sea salt
- Ground black pepper, as required

Directions:

1. In a large non-stick wok, heat half of olive oil over medium heat and stir fry the shrimp for about 1 minute per side.
2. With a slotted spoon, transfer the shrimp onto a plate.
3. In the same wok, heat the remaining oil over medium heat and sauté the onion and garlic for about 2-3 minutes.
4. Add the broccoli, salt and black pepper and stir fry for about 2-3 minutes.
5. Stir in the cooked shrimp and stir fry for about 1-2 minutes.
6. Serve hot.

Shrimp with Zoodles

Servings|4   Time|28 minutes
Nutritional Content (per serving):
Cal| 226   Fat| 8.3g   Protein| 27.4g   Carbs| 7.3g   Fibre| 1.7g

Ingredients:

- 30 millilitres (2 tablespoons) olive oil
- 455 grams (1 pound) shrimp, peeled and deveined
- Ground black pepper, as required
- 2 medium courgettes (zucchinis), spiralized with blade C

- 1 garlic clove, minced
- 1¼ grams (¼ teaspoon) red pepper flakes, crushed
- Pinch of sea salt
- 90 millilitres (1/3 cup) salt-free chicken broth
- 180 grams (1 cup) cherry tomatoes, quartered

Directions:

1. In a large non-stick wok, heat the olive oil over medium heat and sauté garlic and red pepper flakes for about 1 minute.
2. Add shrimp and black pepper and cook for about 1 minute per side.
3. Add broth and zucchini noodles and cook for about 3-4 minutes.
4. Stir in tomato quarters and immediately remove from the heat.
5. Serve hot.

Chickpeas Chili

Servings|5   Time|40 minutes
Nutritional Content (per serving):
Cal| 275   Fat| 5.3g   Protein| 12.4g   Carbs| 44.9g   Fibre| 12.8g

Ingredients:

- ❖ 10 millilitres (2 teaspoons) olive oil
- ❖ 1 carrot , peeled and chopped
- ❖ 2 garlic cloves, minced
- ❖ 5 grams (1 teaspoon) red chili powder
- ❖ Pinch of sea salt
- ❖ 660 grams (4 cups) cooked chickpeas
- ❖ 360 millilitres (1½ cups) water
- ❖ 15 millilitres (1 tablespoon) fresh lemon juice
- ❖ 120 grams (1 cup) onion chopped
- ❖ 1 celery stalk chopped
- ❖ 5 grams (1 teaspoon) paprika
- ❖ 5 grams (1 teaspoon) ground cumin
- ❖ Ground black pepper as required
- ❖ 400 grams (2 cups) tomatoes, chopped finely
- ❖ 5 grams (2 tablespoons) fresh coriander (cilantro) chopped

Directions:

1. In a large saucepan, heat oil over medium heat and sauté onion, carrot, celery and garlic for about 5 minutes.
2. Add spices and sauté for about 1 minute.
3. Add chickpeas, tomatoes, tomato paste and water and bring to a boil.
4. Reduce the heat to low and simmer, covered for about 20 minutes.
5. Stir in lemon juice and cilantro and serve hot.

Chickpeas with Swiss Chard

Servings|4 Time|30 minutes
Nutritional Content (per serving):
Cal| 276   Fat| 9.3g   Protein| 11.4g   Carbs| 37.6g   Fibre| 11.2g

Ingredients:

- ❖ 30 millilitres (2 tablespoons) olive oil
- ❖ 5 grams (1 teaspoon) dried thyme, crushed
- ❖ 2½ grams (½ teaspoon) paprika
- ❖ 415 grams (2½ cups) cooked chickpeas
- ❖ 30 millilitres (2 tablespoons) water
- ❖ Pinch of sea salt
- ❖ 10 grams (2 tablespoons) fresh basil, chopped
- ❖ 1 medium onion, chopped
- ❖ 4 garlic cloves, minced
- ❖ 5 grams (1 teaspoon) dried oregano, crushed
- ❖ 200 grams (1 cup) tomatoes, finely chopped
- ❖ 175 grams (5 cups) Swiss chard, chopped
- ❖ 30 millilitres (2 tablespoons) fresh lemon juice
- ❖ Ground black pepper, as required

Directions:

1. Heat the olive oil in a wok over medium heat and sauté onion for about 6-8 minutes.
2. Add the garlic, herbs and paprika and sauté for about 1 minute.
3. Add the Swiss chard and 30 millilitres (2 tablespoons) of water and cook for about 2-3 minutes.
4. Add the tomatoes and chickpeas and cook for about 2-3 minutes.
5. Add in the lemon juice, salt and black pepper and remove from the heat.
6. Serve hot with the garnishing of basil.

Lentils & Veggie Curry

Servings|8   Time|1¾ hours
Nutritional Content (per serving):
Cal| 160   Fat| 3g   Protein| 7.3g   Carbs| 29.5g   Fibre| 9.8g

Ingredients:

- ❖ 1920 millilitres (8 cups) water
- ❖ 420 grams (2 cups) dry lentils, rinsed
- ❖ 1 large onion, chopped
- ❖ 3 garlic cloves, minced
- ❖ 15 grams (1 tablespoon) curry powder
- ❖ 3 carrots, peeled and chopped
- ❖ 1 Granny Smith apple, cored and chopped
- ❖ 60 grams (2 cups) fresh spinach, chopped
- ❖ Pinch of sea salt
- ❖ 2½ grams (½ teaspoon) ground turmeric
- ❖ 15 millilitres (1 tablespoon) olive oil
- ❖ 2 tomatoes, chopped
- ❖ 10 grams (2 teaspoons) ground cumin
- ❖ 735 grams (3 cups) pumpkin, peeled, seeded and cubed into 1-inch size
- ❖ Ground black pepper, as required

Directions:

1. In a large saucepan, add the water, turmeric and lentils over high heat and bring to a boil.
2. Now, adjust the heat to medium-low and simmer, covered for about 30 minutes.
3. Drain the lentils, reserving 2½ cups of the cooking liquid.
4. Meanwhile, in another large saucepan, heat the oil over medium heat and sauté the onion for about 2-3 minutes.
5. Add in the garlic and sauté for about 1 minute.
6. Add the tomatoes and cook for about 5 minutes.
7. Stir in the curry powder and spices and cook for about 1 minute.
8. Add the carrots, pumpkin, cooked lentils and reserved cooking liquid and bring to a gentle boil.
9. Reduce the heat to medium-low and simmer, covered for about 45 minutes.
10. Stir in the apple and spinach and simmer for about 15 minutes.
11. Stir in the salt and black pepper and serve hot.

Beans & Lentil Chili

Servings|10   Time|1 hour 55 minutes
Nutritional Content (per serving):
Cal| 234   Fat| 6.3g   Protein| 12.4g   Carbs| 33.7g   Fibre| 11.9g

Ingredients:

- 720 grams (4 cups) dried black beans, rinsed
- 2 large capsicums (bell peppers), seeded and chopped
- 25 grams (2 tablespoons) dried oregano
- 15 grams (1 tablespoon) ground cumin
- 800 grams (2 cups) tomatoes, finely chopped
- 1440 millilitres (6 cups) salt-free vegetable broth
- Ground black pepper, as required
- 45 millilitres (3 tablespoons) olive oil
- 3 red onions, chopped
- 3-4 garlic cloves, pressed
- 15 grams (1 tablespoon) ground coriander
- 5 grams (1 teaspoon) paprika
- 105 grams (½ cup) lentils, rinsed
- 480 millilitres (2 cups) homemade tomato puree
- Pinch of sea salt
- 15 grams (½ cup) fresh parsley, chopped

Directions:

1. In a large bowl of water, soak the black beans for about 8 hours.
2. Drain the beans well.
3. In a large deep pan, heat the oil over medium and sauté the capsicums (bell peppers), onions and garlic for about 5 minutes.
4. Add the oregano and spices and sauté for about 3 minutes.
5. Add the beans, lentils, tomatoes, tomato puree and broth and bring to a boil.
6. Adjust the heat to low and simmer, uncovered for about 20-30 minutes.
7. Stir in the corn, salt and black pepper and simmer, uncovered for about 1 hour, stirring occasionally.
8. Serve hot with the garnishing of parsley.

Brown Rice with Beans

Servings|5   Time|1¼ hours
Nutritional Content (per serving):
Cal| 382   Fat| 9.3g   Protein| 12.4g   Carbs| 61g   Fibre| 8.7g

Ingredients:

- ❖ 30 millilitres (2 tablespoons) olive oil
- ❖ 240 grams (1¼ cups) brown rice, rinsed
- ❖ Pinch of sea salt
- ❖ Ground black pepper, as required
- ❖ 4 green onions (scallions), chopped
- ❖ 35 grams (¼ cup) unsalted cashews

- ❖ 2 garlic cloves, minced
- ❖ 200 grams (2 cups) fresh mushrooms, sliced
- ❖ 480 millilitres (2 cups) salt-free vegetable broth
- ❖ 1 capsicum (bell pepper), seeded and chopped
- ❖ 360 grams (2 cups) cooked red kidney beans
- ❖ 5 grams (2 tablespoons) fresh parsley, chopped

Directions:

1. In a large saucepan, heat the oil over medium heat and sauté the onion for about 4-5 minutes.
2. Add the garlic and mushrooms and cook for about 5-6 minutes.
3. Stir in the rice and cook for about 1-2 minutes, stirring continuously.
4. Stir in the broth, salt and black pepper and bring to a boil.
5. Now, adjust the heat to low and simmer, covered for about 35 minutes, stirring occasionally.
6. Add in the bell pepper and beans and cook for about 5-10 minutes or until all the liquid is absorbed.
7. Serve hot with the garnishing of cashews and parsley.

Snacks Recipes

Blueberry Yoghurt Bowl

Servings|2   Time|5 minutes
Nutritional Content (per serving):
Cal| 68   Fat| 0.2g   Protein| 4.5g   Carbs| 12.5g   Fibre| 0.9g

Ingredients:

- ❖ 190 grams (¾ cup) fat-free plain Greek yoghurt
- ❖ 75 grams (½ cup) fresh blueberries

Directions:

1. Divide yoghurt into two serving bowls and top with blueberries
2. Serve immediately.

Berries Gazpacho

Servings|6   Time|10 minutes
Nutritional Content (per serving):
Cal| 61   Fat| 2.8g   Protein| 1.4g   Carbs| 9.1g   Fibre| 4.1g

Ingredients:

- ❖ 210 grams (2 cups) fresh strawberries, hulled and sliced
- ❖ 960 millilitres (4 cups) unsweetened almond milk
- ❖ 250 grams (2 cups) fresh raspberries
- ❖ 2½ millilitres (½ teaspoon) organic vanilla extract

Directions:

1. In a food processor, add all the ingredients and pulse until smooth.
2. Serve immediately.

Salsa Fresca

Servings|8   Time|10 minutes
Nutritional Content (per serving):
Cal| 30   Fat| 1.9g   Protein| 0.7g   Carbs| 3g   Fibre| 0.9g

Ingredients:

- ❖ 455 grams (1 pound) ripe tomatoes, cored and chopped
- ❖ 1 jalapeño pepper, seeded and minced
- ❖ 30 millilitres (2 tablespoons) fresh lemon juice
- ❖ Pinch of sea salt
- ❖ Ground black pepper, as required

- ❖ 2 green onions (scallions), minced
- ❖ 2 garlic cloves, minced
- ❖ 15 millilitres (1 tablespoon) olive oil
- ❖ 15 grams (¼ cup) fresh coriander (cilantro) leaves, chopped

Directions:

1. In a large bowl, add all ingredients and mix until well blended.
2. Cover the bowl and refrigerate for at least 2 hours before serving.

Mango & Cucumber Salsa

Servings|6 Time|15 minutes
Nutritional Content (per serving):
Cal| 40   Fat| 0.3g   Protein| 0.7g   Carbs| 9.7g   Fibre| 1.2g

Ingredients:

- ❖ 1 mango, peeled, pitted and chopped
- ❖ 45 grams (1/3 cup) onion, chopped
- ❖ 15 millilitres (1 tablespoon) fresh lime juice
- ❖ Ground black pepper, as required
- ❖ 75 grams (½ cup) cucumber, peeled and chopped
- ❖ ½ of jalapeño pepper, finely chopped
- ❖ 15 grams (¼ cup) fresh coriander (cilantro) leaves, chopped

Directions:

1. In a large bowl, add all ingredients and mix well.
2. Set aside for about 10-15 minutes before serving.

Fruity Salsa

Servings|8   Time|15 minutes
Nutritional Content (per serving):
Cal| 74   Fat| 0.5g   Protein| 1.1g   Carbs| 18.1g   Fibre| 2.2g

Ingredients:

- 225 grams (8 ounces) fresh pineapple, chopped
- 60 grams (½ cup) onion, chopped
- 15 grams (¼ cup) fresh coriander (cilantro), chopped
- 30 millilitres (2 tablespoons) apple cider vinegar
- 2 large mangoes, peeled, pitted and chopped
- 10 grams (2 teaspoons) fresh ginger, grated finely
- 2½ grams (½ teaspoon) red pepper flakes, crushed
- Pinch of sea salt

Directions:

1. In a large serving bowl, add all ingredients and gently stir to combine.
2. Serve immediately.

Corn & Beans Relish

Servings|8   Time|15 minutes
Nutritional Content (per serving):
Cal| 103   Fat| 0.7g   Protein| 5.5g   Carbs| 20.5g   Fibre| 5.6g

Ingredients:

- 340 grams (2 cups) cooked black beans
- 4 tomatoes, seeded and chopped
- 15 grams (½ cup) fresh parsley, chopped
- 30 millilitres (2 tablespoons) fresh lemon juice
- 125 grams (1 cup) frozen corn kernels, thawed
- 1 capsicum (bell pepper), seeded and chopped
- 2 garlic cloves, chopped
- ½ of medium onion, chopped
- 10 grams (2 teaspoons) coconut sugar

Directions:

1. In a large serving bowl, add all ingredients and gently stir to combine.
2. Refrigerate for at least 30 minutes before serving.

Chickpeas Hummus

Servings|6   Time|15 minutes
Nutritional Content (per serving):
Cal| 190   Fat| 11.3g   Protein| 5.2g   Carbs| 15.9g   Fibre| 3.8g

Ingredients:

- ❖ 80 grams (¼ cup) tahini
- ❖ 1 small garlic clove, minced
- ❖ 30 millilitres (2 tablespoons) olive oil
- ❖ 330 grams (2 cups) cooked chickpeas
- ❖ Pinch of paprika
- ❖ 60 millilitres (¼ cup) fresh lemon juice
- ❖ 2½ grams (½ teaspoon) ground cumin
- ❖ 30-45 millilitres (2-3 tablespoons) water

Directions:

1. In a food processor, add tahini and lemon juice and pule for about 1 minute.
2. Scrape the sides and bottom of food processor and pulse for about 30 seconds more.
3. Add the garlic, 2 tablespoons of olive oil and cumin and pulse for about 30 seconds
4. Scrape the sides and bottom of food processor and pulse for about 30 seconds more.
5. Add half of the chickpeas and pulse for about 1 minute.
6. Scrape sides and bottom of food processor.
7. Add remaining chickpeas and pulse for about 1-2 minutes or until just smooth.
8. Add water and pulse until smooth.
9. Transfer hummus into a serving bowl.
10. Sprinkle with paprika and serve.

Chickpeas & Carrot Hummus

Servings|8   Time|45 minutes
Nutritional Content (per serving):
Cal| 131   Fat| 7.3g   Protein| 3.1g   Carbs| 13.1g   Fibre| 3g

Ingredients:

- ❖ 3 carrots, peeled and roughly chopped
- ❖ 5 grams (1 teaspoon) paprika, divided
- ❖ 30 grams (1½ tablespoons) tahini
- ❖ 2½ grams (½ teaspoon) ground cumin
- ❖ 45 millilitres (3 tablespoons) olive oil, divided
- ❖ 1 garlic clove, peeled
- ❖ 330 grams (2 cups) cooked chickpeas
- ❖ 30 millilitres (2 tablespoons) fresh lemon juice
- ❖ 90 millilitres (1/3 cup) water

Directions:

1. Preheat your oven to 200 ⁰C (400 ⁰F).
2. Place the carrots, 15 millilitres (1 tablespoon) of oil, 1½ grams (½ teaspoon) of paprika and a pinch of sea salt and toss to coat well.
3. Then, spread the carrot pieces in an even layer.
4. Bake for approximately 25 minutes.
5. Place the garlic clove onto the baking sheet with carrot pieces and bake for approximately 10 minutes.
6. Remove from the oven and set aside to cool.
7. In a food processor, add the carrot, garlic and remaining ingredients and pulse until smooth.
8. Serve immediately.

Beans & Cauliflower Hummus

Servings|10   Time|10 minutes
Nutritional Content (per serving):
Cal| 97   Fat| 4.1g   Protein| 4.7g   Carbs| 11.9g   Fibre| 3.4g

Ingredients:

- ❖ 140 grams (5 ounces) cooked black beans
- ❖ 60 grams (3 tablespoons) tahini
- ❖ 5 grams (1 teaspoon) ground cumin
- ❖ 5 grams (2 tablespoons) fresh parsley, chopped
- ❖ 65 grams (¼ cup) salsa
- ❖ 2 garlic cloves, chopped
- ❖ 200 grams (2 cups) cooked cauliflower
- ❖ 5 millilitres (1 teaspoon) olive oil

Directions:

1. In a high-power blender, add all ingredients except for parsley and pulse until smooth.
2. Garnish with parsley and serve.

Black Beans Dip

Servings|4   Time|19 minutes
Nutritional Content (per serving):
Cal| 163   Fat| 4g   Protein| 8.4g   Carbs| 24g   Fibre| 8.4g

Ingredients:

- ❖ 15 millilitres (1 tablespoon) olive oil
- ❖ 385 grams (2¼ cups) cooked black beans
- ❖ 15 millilitres (1 tablespoon) fresh lime juice
- ❖ Pinch of sea salt
- ❖ 1 garlic clove, chopped
- ❖ 5 grams (1 teaspoon) fresh ginger, chopped
- ❖ 30-45 millilitres (2-3 tablespoons) water
- ❖ Ground black pepper, as required

Directions:

1. In a small frying pan, heat the oil over medium-low heat and sauté the garlic and ginger for about 1-2 minutes.
2. Add the black beans and 2-3 tablespoons of water and cook for about 2 minutes.
3. Remove from the heat and stir in the lime juice, salt and black pepper.
4. With a potato masher, mash until smooth.
5. Serve immediately.

Spinach Dip

Servings|8   Time|17 minutes
Nutritional Content (per serving):
Cal| 88   Fat| 6g   Protein| 4.8g   Carbs| 4.5g   Fibre| 0.9g

Ingredients:

- ❖ 285 grams (10 ounces) fresh baby spinach
- ❖ 250 grams (1 cup) fat-free plain Greek yoghurt, drained well
- ❖ 25 grams (¼ cup) green onions (scallions), finely chopped
- ❖ 1 garlic clove, minced
- ❖ 115 grams (4 ounces) fat-free cream cheese, softened
- ❖ 30 grams (¼ cup) low-fat Parmesan cheese, grated
- ❖ 15 millilitres (1 tablespoon) fresh lemon juice

Directions:

1. In a large pan of boiling water, cook the spinach for about 1-2 minutes or until just wilted.
2. Drain the spinach well and then squeeze to remove any liquid.
3. Then chop the spinach finely.
4. In a large bowl, add cream cheese and yoghurt and stir until smooth.
5. Add the spinach and remaining ingredients and mix until well blended.
6. Refrigerate before serving.

Beans & Veggie Dip

Servings|8   Time|45 minutes
Nutritional Content (per serving):
Cal| 84   Fat| 1.6g   Protein| 5.3g   Carbs| 13.8g   Fibre| 4.8g

Ingredients:

- ❖ 1 (425 grams) (15 ounces) can artichoke hearts in water, drained
- ❖ 5 grams (1 teaspoon) ground black pepper
- ❖ 2½ grams (½ teaspoon) dried thyme
- ❖ 15 grams (2 tablespoons) low-fat Parmesan cheese, grated

- ❖ 120 grams (4 cups) fresh spinach, chopped
- ❖ 2 garlic cloves, minced
- ❖ 5 grams (1 teaspoon) dried parsley
- ❖ 180 grams (1 cup) cooked white beans
- ❖ 120 grams (½ cup) low-fat sour cream

Directions:

1. Preheat your oven to 180 °C (350 °F).
2. In a large bowl, add all ingredients and mix until well combined.
3. Place the mixture into a baking dish and spread in an even layer.
4. Bake for about 30 minutes.
5. Serve warm.

Brinjal Caviar

Servings|4   Time|35 minutes
Nutritional Content (per serving):
Cal| 81   Fat| 3.9g   Protein| 2.1g   Carbs| 11.7g   Fibre| 6.4g

Ingredients:

- 680 grams (2½ pounds) brinjals (eggplants), halved lengthwise
- 5 grams (2 teaspoons) fresh basil leaves
- 15 millilitres (1 tablespoon) fresh lemon juice
- 15 millilitres (1 tablespoon) olive oil
- 2 small garlic cloves, roughly chopped
- 50 grams (½ cup) green onion (scallion), chopped
- 30 millilitres (2 tablespoons) salt-free vegetable broth

Directions:

1. Preheat your oven to 200 ºC (400 ºF). Grease a baking sheet.
2. Place brinjal (eggplant) halves onto the prepared baking sheet, cut-side facing down.
3. Roast for about 20 minutes.
4. Remove from the oven and let them cool slightly.
5. With a spoon, scoop out the pulp from skin.
6. In a food processor, add eggplant pulp and remaining ingredients except for oil and pulse until smooth.
7. Transfer the caviar into a bowl.
8. Add the olive oil and stir to combine.
9. Serve at room temperature.

Cucumber Cups

Servings|10   Time|15 minutes
Nutritional Content (per serving):
Cal| 51   Fat| 3.9g   Protein| 0.8g   Carbs| 4.4g   Fibre| 1.2g

Ingredients:

- 2 English cucumbers
- 25 grams (3 tablespoons) onion, finely chopped
- 10 grams (1 tablespoon) fresh lemon zest, grated finely
- 5 grams (2 tablespoons) fresh tarragon, finely chopped
- 225 grams (1½ cups) olives, pitted and finely chopped
- ½ of small jalapeño pepper, seeded and minced finely
- 2 garlic cloves, minced finely
- 15 millilitres (1 tablespoon) olive oil

Directions:

1. Cut each cucumber into 1¼-centimetre (½-inch) thin rounds.
2. Carefully scoop out half of the seedbed from each slice.
3. In a large bowl, mix together all ingredients except for cucumber cups.
4. Scoop the mixture in each cucumber cup evenly.
5. Serve immediately.

Tomato Bruschetta

Servings|6   Time|19 minutes
Nutritional Content (per serving):
Cal| 100   Fat| 2.4g   Protein| 3.7g   Carbs| 16.3g   Fibre| 3g

Ingredients:

- ½ of whole-wheat baguette, cut into 6 slices diagonally
- 2 garlic cloves, minced
- 5 grams (2 tablespoons) fresh parsley, chopped
- 5 millilitres (1 teaspoon) olive oil
- 3 tomatoes, chopped
- 60 grams (½ cup) onion, chopped
- 10 millilitres (2 teaspoons) balsamic vinegar
- Ground black pepper, as required

Directions:

1. Preheat your oven to broiler.
2. Arrange a rack in the top portion of the oven.
3. Arrange the bread slices onto a baking sheet in a single layer.
4. Broil for about 2 minutes per side.
5. Meanwhile in a bowl, add remaining ingredients and toss to coat.
6. Place the tomato mixture on each toasted bread slice evenly and serve immediately.

Stuffed Mushrooms

Servings|20   Time|35 minutes
Nutritional Content (per serving):
Cal| 88   Fat| 4.9g   Protein| 4.4g   Carbs| 8.5g   Fibre| 1.3g

Ingredients:

- ❖ 60 grams (2 cups) fresh basil leaves
- ❖ 15 grams (2 tablespoons) unsalted pumpkin seeds
- ❖ 10 millilitres (2 teaspoons) fresh lemon juice
- ❖ 150 grams (1½ cups) whole-wheat breadcrumbs
- ❖ 20 fresh cremini mushrooms, stems removed
- ❖ 2 garlic cloves, peeled
- ❖ 30 grams (¼ cup) low-fat Parmesan cheese, shredded
- ❖ 75 millilitres (5 tablespoon) olive oil, divided
- ❖ Pinch of sea salt
- ❖ 10 grams (2 tablespoons) fresh parsley, chopped

Directions:

3. Preheat your oven to 180 °C (350 °F).
4. For filling: in a food processor, place the basil, garlic, cheese, pumpkin seeds, 15 millilitres (1 tablespoon) of oil, lemon juice and salt and pulse until smooth.
5. For topping: in a small bowl, blend together the remaining oil, breadcrumbs and parsley and mix well.
6. Arrange the mushroom caps onto a baking sheet, upside down.
7. Stuff each mushroom cap with the filling mixture and sprinkle with topping mixture.
8. Bake for 10-15 minutes or until golden brown.
9. Serve warm.

Butternut Squash Fries

Servings|6   Time|30 minutes
Nutritional Content (per serving):
Cal| 91   Fat| 2.7g   Protein| 1.6g   Carbs| 18.2g   Fibre| 3.4g

Ingredients:

❖ 1 medium butternut squash, peeled, seeded and cut into sticks
❖ Pinch of sea salt

❖ 5 grams (2 tablespoons) fresh rosemary, chopped
❖ 15 millilitres (1 tablespoon) olive oil

Directions:

1. Preheat your oven to 220 ºC (425 ºF). Lightly grease a baking sheet.
2. In a bowl, add all ingredients and toss to coat well.
3. Arrange squash sticks onto prepared baking sheet in a single layer.
4. Roast for about 10 minutes.
5. Flip and roast for about 5-10 minutes or until golden brown.
6. Serve hot.

Potato Sticks

Servings|2   Time|25 minutes
Nutritional Content (per serving):
Cal| 131   Fat| 7.4g   Protein| 1.9g   Carbs| 15.6g   Fibre| 2.2g

Ingredients:

- 1 large russet potato, peeled and cut into 1/8-inch thick sticks lengthwise
- 1¼ grams (¼ teaspoon) red chili powder
- Pinch of sea salt
- 10 curry leaves
- 1¼ grams (¼ teaspoon) ground turmeric
- 15 millilitres (1 tablespoon) olive oil

Directions:

1. Preheat your oven to 200 ºC (400 ºF). Line 2 baking sheets with parchment papers.
2. In a large bowl, add all ingredients and toss to coat well.
3. Transfer the mixture into prepared baking sheets in a single layer.
4. Bake for about 10 minutes.
5. Serve immediately.

Chicken Nuggets

Servings|8   Time|45 minutes
Nutritional Content (per serving):
Cal| 157   Fat| 8.3g   Protein| 14.5g   Carbs| 2.8g   Fibre| 1.6g

Ingredients:

- ❖ 2 (225-gram) (8-ounce) skinless, boneless chicken breasts
- ❖ 2½ grams (½ teaspoon) paprika
- ❖ Ground black pepper, as required

- ❖ 4 egg whites
- ❖ 100 grams (1 cup) almond flour
- ❖ 5 grams (1 teaspoon) dried oregano, crushed
- ❖ Pinch of sea salt

Directions:

1. Cut each chicken breast into 5x2½-centimetre (2x1-inch) chunks
2. In a bowl, whisk the egg whites well.
3. Place the flour, oregano, paprika, salt, and black pepper in another shallow bowl and mix until well combined.
4. Dip the chicken nuggets in beaten eggs and then, evenly coat with the flour mixture.
5. Arrange the chicken nuggets onto the prepared baking sheet in a single layer.
6. Bake for about 30 minutes or until golden brown.
7. Serve warm.

Crispy Shrimp

Servings|6   Time|40 minutes
Nutritional Content (per serving):
Cal| 175   Fat| 7.3g   Protein| 19.3g   Carbs| 5.1g   Fibre| 2g

Ingredients:

- ❖ 25 grams (¼ cup) almond flour
- ❖ Ground black pepper, as required
- ❖ 455 grams (1 pound) shrimp, peeled and deveined
- ❖ Pinch of sea salt
- ❖ 2 large egg whites
- ❖ 70 grams (1 cup) low-fat unsweetened coconut flakes

Directions:

1. Preheat your oven to 200 ºC (400 ºF). Grease a large baking sheet.
2. Place the coconut flour, salt and black pepper in a shallow bowl and mix until well combined.
3. Place the egg whites in a second bowl and beat well.
4. Add the coconut flakes in a third bowl.
5. Coat the shrimp with flour, then dip into the beaten egg whites and finally, coat with coconut flakes.
6. Arrange the shrimp onto the prepared baking sheet in a single layer.
7. Bake for about 15 minutes.
8. Remove the baking sheet from oven and flip the shrimp.
9. Now, set the oven to broiler.
10. Broil the shrimp for about 3-5 minutes
11. Serve warm.

Spiced Shrimp

Servings|5   Time|25 minutes
Nutritional Content (per serving):
Cal| 123   Fat| 20.6g   Protein| 2.4g   Carbs| 2.9g   Fibre| 0.6g

Ingredients:

- ❖ 455 grams (1 pound) shrimp, peeled and deveined
- ❖ 10 millilitres (2 teaspoons) water
- ❖ 2½ grams (½ teaspoon) red chili powder
- ❖ 20 grams (2 tablespoons) homemade tomato paste
- ❖ 5 millilitres (1 teaspoon) olive oil
- ❖ 1 small garlic clove, minced
- ❖ 2½ grams (½ teaspoon) dried oregano

Directions:

1. For marinade: in a bowl, add all ingredients except for shrimp and mx well.
2. Add the shrimp and coat with marinade evenly.
3. Refrigerate for about 30 minutes.
4. Preheat the broiler of oven. Arrange a rack about 10-centimetre (4-inch) from heating element.
5. Lightly grease a broiler pan.
6. Arrange the shrimp onto the prepared broiler pan in a single layer.
7. Broil for about 3-4 minutes per side.
8. Serve warm.

Beverages Recipes

Lemonade

Servings|4   Time|10 minutes
Nutritional Content (per serving):
Cal| 11   Fat| 0.4g   Protein| 0.4g   Carbs| 1g   Fibre| 0.2g

Ingredients:

- ❖ 180 millilitres (¾ cup) fresh lemon juice
- ❖ 840 millilitres (3½ cups) cold water
- ❖ 30 grams (2 tablespoons) maple syrup
- ❖ Ice cubes, as required

Directions:

1. In a large pitcher, mix together the lemon juice and stevia.
2. Add the water and fill the pitcher with ice.
3. Serve chilled.

Tea Lemonade

Servings|8   Time|10 minutes
Nutritional Content (per serving):
Cal| 92   Fat| 0.3g   Protein| 0.3g   Carbs| 23.3g   Fibre| 0.2g

Ingredients:

- 6 orange spice tea bags
- 960 millilitres (4 cups) boiling water
- 240 millilitres (1 cup) fresh lemon juice
- 1 lemon, cut into slices
- 180 grams (1 cup) coconut sugar
- 480 millilitres (2 cups) cold water
- Ice cubes, as required

Directions:

4. In a pitcher, add tea bags and sugar.
5. Add boiling water and stir until sugar dissolves. Set aside to cool.
6. Remove tea bags and stir in cold water and lemon juice.
7. Refrigerate to chill for about 2 hours.
8. Fill serving glasses with ice cubes.
9. Pour chilled tea and serve with the garnishing of lemon slices.

Blueberry Lemonade

Servings|16   Time|20 minutes
Nutritional Content (per serving):
Cal| 20   Fat| 0.2g   Protein| 0.2g   Carbs| 4.6g   Fibre| 0.3g

Ingredients:

- 480 millilitres (2 cups) water, divided
- 10 grams (1 tablespoon) dried lavender flowers
- 240 millilitres (1 cup) fresh lemon juice
- 150 grams (6 ounces) fresh blueberries
- 45 grams (¼ cup) coconut sugar
- Ice cubes, as required
- Cold water, as required

Directions:

1. In a medium saucepan, add 2 cups of water and bring to a boil.
2. Add the blueberries, lavender and coconut sugar and boil for about 5 minutes, stirring occasionally.
3. in a large pitcher, place the ice.
4. Through a fine-mesh sieve, strain blueberry the mixture into the pitcher
5. Add the lemon juice and enough cold water to fill to the top and mix well.
6. Serve chilled.

Cranberry Spritzer

Servings|10   Time|10 minutes
Nutritional Content (per serving):
Cal| 67   Fat| 0.4g   Protein| 0.3g   Carbs| 13.7g   Fibre| 2g

Ingredients:

- 960 millilitres (4 cups) chilled seltzer water
- 120 millilitres (½ cup) chilled fresh lemon juice
- 45 grams (¼ cup) coconut sugar
- 960 millilitres (4 cups) chilled fresh cranberry juice
- 150 grams (1 cup) raspberry sherbet
- 2 lemons, cut into wedges

Directions:

1. In a large pitcher, add all ingredients and mix well.
2. Transfer into chilled glasses and serve with the garnishing of lemon wedges.

Fruity Agua Fresca

Servings|6   Time|10 minutes
Nutritional Content (per serving):
Cal| 49   Fat| 0.2g   Protein| 0.7g   Carbs| 1.1g   Fibre| 0.5g

Ingredients:

- 680 grams (2½ pounds) seedless watermelon, peeled and chopped
- 1 lime, cut into 6 slices
- 240 millilitres (1 cup) unsweetened cranberry juice
- 60 millilitres (¼ cup) fresh lime juice

Directions:

1. In a high-power blender, add the watermelon and pulse until smooth.
2. Through a fine-mesh sieve, strain the watermelon puree into a large pitcher.
3. Add the cranberry and lime juices and stir to combine.
4. Refrigerate until chilled.
5. Pour into tall chilled glasses and serve with the garnishing of lime slices.

Strawberry Mockarita

Servings|6   Time|10 minutes
Nutritional Content (per serving):
Cal| 51   Fat| 0.2g   Protein| 0.5g   Carbs| 13g   Fibre| 1.4g

Ingredients:

- ❖ 420 grams (4 cups) fresh strawberries, hulled and sliced
- ❖ 45 grams (¼ cup) coconut sugar
- ❖ 60 millilitres (¼ cup) fresh lime juice
- ❖ 480 millilitres (2 cups) water
- ❖ Ice cubes, as required

Directions:

1. Place all of the ingredients in a high-power blender and pulse until smooth.
2. Serve immediately.

Citrus Mockarita

Servings|2   Time|10 minutes
Nutritional Content (per serving):
Cal| 126   Fat| 0.2g   Protein| 0.3g   Carbs| 30.6g   Fibre| 0.1g

Ingredients:

- 155 millilitres (2/3 cup) fresh lime juice
- 75 grams (¼ cup) maple syrup
- Ice cubes, as required
- 90 millilitres (1/3 cup) fresh orange juice
- 240 millilitres (1 cup) chilled lime seltzer

Directions:

1. In a bowl, add the lime juice, orange juice and maple syrup and mix well.
2. Transfer the fruit mixture into ice cube trays and freeze until set.
3. In a high-power blender, add juice cubes, seltzer and ice cubes and pulse until smooth.
4. Serve immediately.

Fruit Mocktail

Servings|16 Time|10 minutes
Nutritional Content (per serving):
Cal| 63   Fat| 0.2g   Protein| 0.7g   Carbs| 15.9g   Fibre| 1.8g

Ingredients:

- ❖ 2 (285 grams) (10 ounces) bags unsweetened frozen strawberries
- ❖ 1920 millilitres (8 cups) chilled carbonated water

- ❖ 850 grams (30 ounces) canned crushed pineapple with juice
- ❖ 720 millilitres (3 cups) fresh orange juice (with pulp)
- ❖ 2 cups fresh strawberries, hulled

Directions:

1. In a high-power blender, add the frozen strawberries, crushed pineapple and orange juice and pulse until smooth and foamy.
2. Transfer the fruit mixture into silicone ice cube trays.
3. Freeze the ice cube trays until set.
4. Divide fruity cubes into serving tall glasses and fill each with carbonated water.
5. Set aside for about5 minutes before serving.
6. Garnish with strawberries and serve.

Apple & Lemon Punch

Servings|4   Time|10 minutes
Nutritional Content (per serving):
Cal| 60   Fat| 0.2g   Protein| 0.1g   Carbs| 14.6g   Fibre| 0.1g

Ingredients:

- ❖ 480 millilitres (2 cups) unsweetened apple juice
- ❖ 480 millilitres (2 cups) lemon-flavored sparkling water
- ❖ 10 millilitres (2 teaspoons) fresh lemon juice

Directions:

1. In a pitcher, add all ingredients and stir to combine.
2. Transfer into chilled glasses and serve.

Pineapple Punch

Servings|6   Time|10 minutes
Nutritional Content (per serving):
Cal| 61   Fat| 0.2g   Protein| 0.9g   Carbs| 14.6g   Fibre| 2.8g

Ingredients:

- ❖ 255 grams (1½ cups) fresh pineapple, chopped
- ❖ 240 millilitres (1 cup) fresh cranberry juice
- ❖ Ice cubes, as required
- ❖ 2 oranges, peeled, seeded and sectioned
- ❖ 30 millilitres (2 tablespoons) fresh lemon juice

Directions:

1. Place all ingredients except for ice in a high-power blender and pulse until smooth.
2. Add about 12-14 ice cubes and pulse until smooth.
3. Serve over ice.

Iced Latte

Servings|4   Time|10 minutes
Nutritional Content (per serving):
Cal| 99   Fat| 3.3g   Protein| 3.7g   Carbs| 12.6g   Fibre| 0g

Ingredients:

- ❖ 480 millilitres (2 cups) brewed and cooled decaffeinated espresso coffee
- ❖ 20 grams (2 tablespoons) sugar-free almond syrup
- ❖ 5 grams (1 teaspoon) ground espresso beans
- ❖ 25 grams (2 tablespoons) golden brown sugar
- ❖ 360 millilitres (1½ cups) fat-free milk
- ❖ Ice cubes, as required
- ❖ 60 grams (½ cup) fat-free whipped topping

Directions:

1. In a pitcher, add the cooled coffee, brown sugar, milk and almond syrup and stir to combine.
2. Refrigerate the pitcher to cool completely.
3. Place ice cubes into 4 serving glasses and pour in the coffee mixture.
4. Top each glass with whipped topping evenly.
5. Serve immediately with the sprinkling of ground espresso beans.

Mint Ice Tea

Servings|1   Time|10 minutes
Nutritional Content (per serving):
Cal| 26   Fat| 0.1g   Protein| 0.5g   Carbs| 7g   Fibre| 1.2g

Ingredients:

- ❖ 240 millilitres (1 cup) freshly brewed unsweetened tea, cooled
- ❖ 10 grams (2 tablespoons) fresh mint leaves
- ❖ 5-6 ice cubes
- ❖ 20 grams (2 tablespoons) lime juice concentrate
- ❖ 5 grams (1 teaspoon) maple syrup

Directions:

1. In a high-power blender, add all ingredients and pulse until smooth and frothy.
2. Transfer into serving glasses and serve.

Strawberry Iced Tea

Servings|6   Time|15 minutes
Nutritional Content (per serving):
Cal| 32   Fat| 0.2g   Protein| 0.6g   Carbs| 7.6g   Fibre| 1g

Ingredients:

- 1920 millilitres (8 cups) water
- 225 grams (8 ounces) fresh strawberries, hulled
- 5 grams (1 teaspoon) lime zest, grated
- 8 green tea bags
- 240 millilitres (1 cup) fresh orange juice
- 1 lime, sliced

Directions:

1. In a saucepan, add 1920 millilitres (8 cups) of water on high heat and bring to a boil.
2. In a pitcher, add tea bags.
3. Add boiling water and brew, covered for about 5 minutes.
4. Remove tea bags and refrigerate to chill.
5. In a food processor, add strawberries and pulse until roughly chopped.
6. In a bowl, mix together strawberries, orange juice and lime zest.
7. Transfer the mixture into ice cube trays and freeze for about 2 hours.
8. For serving: fill the tall serving glasses with strawberry ice cubes.
9. Pour chilled green tea and serve immediately with the garnishing of lime slices.

Blackberry Ice Tea

Servings|6   Time|15 minutes
Nutritional Content (per serving):
Cal| 39   Fat| 0.1g   Protein| 0.2g   Carbs| 9.4g   Fibre| 0.2g

Ingredients:

- ❖ 1440 millilitres (6 cups) water
- ❖ 10 grams (2 teaspoons) fresh ginger, minced
- ❖ 45 grams (3 tablespoons) maple syrup
- ❖ 12 blackberry herbal tea bags
- ❖ 2 cinnamon sticks
- ❖ 240 millilitres (1 cup) unsweetened cranberry juice
- ❖ Crushed ice, as required

Directions:

1. In a large saucepan, add water and bring to a boil.
2. Add tea bags, ginger and cinnamon sticks and immediately cover the pan.
3. Remove from heat and steep, covered for about 15 minutes.
4. Through a fine-mesh sieve, strain the mixture into a pitcher.
5. Add the cranberry juice and maple syrup and stir to combine.
6. Refrigerate to chill.
7. Fill 6 serving glasses with crushed ice.
8. Pour the tea over the ice and serve immediately.

Banana Smoothie

Servings|2   Time|10 minutes
Nutritional Content (per serving):
Cal| 128   Fat| 6g   Protein| 2.7g   Carbs| 16.9g   Fibre| 3.2g

Ingredients:

- ❖ 480 millilitres (2 cups) chilled unsweetened almond milk
- ❖ 10 grams (1 tablespoon) unsalted almonds, chopped
- ❖ 1 large frozen banana, peeled and sliced
- ❖ 5 millilitres (1 teaspoon) organic vanilla extract

Directions:

1. Add all the ingredients in a high-power blender and pulse until smooth.
2. Pour the smoothie into two glasses and serve immediately.

Strawberry Smoothie

Servings|2   Time|10 minutes
Nutritional Content (per serving):
Cal| 122   Fat| 3.6g   Protein| 1.7g   Carbs| 22.7g   Fibre| 4.2g

Ingredients:

- ❖ 480 millilitres (2 cups) chilled unsweetened almond milk
- ❖ 1¼ millilitres (¼ teaspoon) organic vanilla extract
- ❖ 165 grams (1½ cups) frozen strawberries
- ❖ 1 banana, peeled and sliced

Directions:

1. Add all the ingredients in a high-power blender and pulse until smooth.
2. Pour the smoothie into two glasses and serve immediately.

Berries & Spinach Smoothie

Servings|2   Time|10 minutes
Nutritional Content (per serving):
Cal| 178   Fat| 4.3g   Protein| 11.2g   Carbs| 23.2g   Fibre| 9.3g

Ingredients:

- ❖ 190 grams (1½ cups) frozen mixed berries
- ❖ 45 grams (3 tablespoons) hemp protein powder
- ❖ 60 grams (2 cups) fresh spinach
- ❖ 1 celery stalk, chopped
- ❖ 300 millilitres (1¼ cups) unsweetened almond milk

Directions:

1. Add all the ingredients in a high-power blender and pulse until smooth.
2. Pour the smoothie into two glasses and serve immediately.

21 Days Action Plan

Day 1:

Breakfast: Spinach Omelet

Mid-Morning Snack: Lemonade

Lunch: Turkey Burgers

Afternoon Snack: Mango & Cucumber Salsa

Dinner: Parsley Salmon

Day 2:

Breakfast: Blueberry Muffins

Mid-Morning Snack: Citrus Mockarita

Lunch: Beet Salad

Afternoon Snack: Beans & Cauliflower Hummus

Dinner: Oregano Chicken Breasts

Day 3:

Breakfast: Courgette Bread

Mid-Morning Snack: Fruity Agua Fresca

Lunch: Broccoli & Spinach Soup

Afternoon Snack: Brinjal Caviar

Dinner: Ground Turkey with Mushrooms

Day 4:

Breakfast: Chicken Pancakes

Mid-Morning Snack: Mint Ice Tea

Lunch: Chickpeas Falafel

Afternoon Snack: Stuffed Mushrooms

Dinner: Lentils & Veggie Curry

Day 5:

Breakfast: Fruity Chia Pudding

Mid-Morning Snack:

Lunch: Stuffed Sweet Potato

Afternoon Snack: Spiced Shrimp

Dinner: Chicken with Pears

Day 6:

Breakfast: Cinnamon Waffles

Mid-Morning Snack: Fruit Mocktail

Lunch: Quinoa with Green Peas

Afternoon Snack: Salsa Fresca

Dinner: Mixed Beans Soup

Day 7:

Breakfast: Tuna Omelet

Mid-Morning Snack: Iced Latte

Lunch: Tofu with Brussels Sprout

Afternoon Snack: Cucumber Cups

Dinner: Shrimp with Broccoli

Day 8:

Breakfast: Overnight Oatmeal

Mid-Morning Snack: Cranberry Spritzer

Lunch: Raspberry Salad

Afternoon Snack: Chickpeas & Carrot Hummus

Dinner: Ground Turkey with Green Peas

Day 9:

Breakfast: Chicken Muffins

Mid-Morning Snack: Strawberry Ice Tea

Lunch: Tofu Lettuce Wraps

Afternoon Snack: Potato Sticks

Dinner: Beans & Lentil Chili

Day 10:

Breakfast: Quinoa Bread

Mid-Morning Snack: Banana Smoothie

Lunch: Beans & Quinoa Burgers

Afternoon Snack: Butternut Squash Fries

Dinner: Stuffed Chicken Breasts

Day 11:

Breakfast: Blueberry Toasts

Mid-Morning Snack: Berries & Spinach Smoothie

Lunch: Lentil Falafel

Afternoon Snack: Crispy Shrimp

Dinner: Chicken with Capsicums

Day 12:

Breakfast: Veggie Muffins

Mid-Morning Snack: Tea Lemonade

Lunch: Beans & Oat Falafel

Afternoon Snack: Fruity Salsa

Dinner: Sweet & Sour Salmon

Day 13:

Breakfast: Spinach Pancakes

Mid-Morning Snack: Iced Latte

Lunch: Courgette & Tomato Salad

Afternoon Snack: Berries Gazpacho

Dinner: Rice with Beans

Day 14:

Breakfast: Tomato Omelet

Mid-Morning Snack: Fruity Agua Fresca

Lunch: Squash & Apple Soup

Afternoon Snack: Chicken Nuggets

Dinner: Chickpeas with Swiss Chard

Day 15:

Breakfast: Yoghurt Oatmeal

Mid-Morning Snack: Strawberry Mockarita

Lunch: Quinoa with Mushroom

Afternoon Snack: Beans & Veggie Dip

Dinner: White Beans & Kale Soup

Day 16:

Breakfast: Vanilla Waffles

Mid-Morning Snack: Pineapple Punch

Lunch: Tofu with Green Peas

Afternoon Snack: Chickpeas Hummus

Dinner: Chicken with Broccoli

Day 17:

Breakfast: Apple Porridge

Mid-Morning Snack: Strawberry Smoothie

Lunch: Turkey Meatballs

Afternoon Snack: Spinach Dip

Dinner: Shrimp with Zoodles

Day 18:

Breakfast: Banana Pancakes

Mid-Morning Snack: Blackberry Ice Tea

Lunch: Shrimp Lettuce Wraps

Afternoon Snack: Tomato Bruschetta

Dinner: Chickpeas Chili

Day 19:

Breakfast: Tomato & Egg Scramble

Mid-Morning Snack: Blueberry Lemonade

Lunch: Lentil Burgers

Afternoon Snack: Corn & Beans Relish

Dinner: Shrimp with Capsicums

Day 20:

Breakfast: Blueberry Bread

Mid-Morning Snack: Apple & Lemon Punch

Lunch: Cauliflower with Green Peas

Afternoon Snack: Black Beans Dip

Dinner: Turkey & Lentil Soup

Day 21:

Breakfast: Buckwheat Porridge

Mid-Morning Snack: Cranberry Spritzer

Lunch: Strawberry Salad

Afternoon Snack: Blueberry Yoghurt Bowl

Dinner: Chicken with Mushroom Sauce

Index

Printed in Great Britain
by Amazon

21449510R00077